BREAKING PASSIVE-AGGRESSIVE CYCLES ~
The Silent Cry of Christian Women

DEE BROWN

Dedication &
Special Acknowledgments

I thank the Holy Spirit for giving me the messages in this book to minister to the daughters, in the world, who need to be set free from chains of oppression and various forms of abuse. I could not have done it without His prompting, leading and guidance. I am humbled by the way He has expressed His love for the women who have cried out or cried silently. Now, I understand the many times the Holy Spirit woke me in the midnight hours with specific women on my mind and instructed me to write specific words to speak directly to their hearts. May the kingdom of God be glorified!

I affectionately dedicate this book to women all over the world who are living in, or are struggling with, abusive relationships. Yet, their persevering spirit is to be admired and shouted from the mountain tops. I pray this book will impart a sense of validation to those who have been crushed, abused, accused or misused. Women, you are precious and can declare that you are more than a conqueror. I honor and value all the knowledge, I have learned from the women's stories, as they opened up broken hearts to break the silent cry of abuse and passive aggression. Your desires to break free and walk in liberty, as the daughters of the Almighty God, with a royal lineage have been heard. My sisters, may I do justice to giving voice to the silent cry deep within you.

I want to specifically give my respect, admiration and my love to my daughter, Tasha Nitika Brown, whose wisdom, practical insights and sensitivity to the Holy Spirit go beyond her years. She has been instrumental in me writing three books. She consistently reminded me of the Holy assignment the Abba Father called me to fulfill. When I started writing this book, I thought I should include various topics and I merrily went about fulfilling that intent. I will never forget the day I was sharing with my daughter. I can still hear her voice saying, "Mom, there are lots of topics you could put into the book, but are they what God told you to write? Mom, you must keep it simple, keep it practical and keep it real." Many times that statement has proven to be the guiding force to stay focused. Her discerning, balanced statement consistently reminded me to stay in tune to the Holy Spirit's voice, as well as, redirected me back to the original purpose of this book. Thank you so much, Tasha, for your genuine love, prayers and accountability. I am privileged to be your mother.

I especially acknowledge Diane Altman. You are my friend, a prayer warrior, and an extraordinary editor. I will be eternally grateful for your uncompromised commitment to see this Holy assignment completed with integrity, professionalism and personal dedication. When the Abba Father called me to write about the battles of spiritual warfare and the victory promised, you supported me through the journey. Although, Diane is a wife, homeschooling mother, an executive business coach, cheerleading coach and an ordained pastor, she said yes to edit this book. I am thankful to God for giving you seasonal breaks to complete this assignment. I pray God continues to pour out His blessings and anoints you to fulfill all called future endeavors. You are dearly loved.

Finally, I want to give a special dedication in memory of, and love for, my mother Bessie Williamson. I will always remember you telling me to put my thoughts to pen and paper.

~ *Encouragement and Inspiration* ~

Breaking Passive-Aggressive Cycles ~
The Silent Cry of Christian Women

The insights in this book will release a renewed hope that healing, liberty and restoration is possible. You will discover a path to help you understand, identify and change unhealthy interactions with passive-aggressive people by God's grace and wisdom. You do not have to journey alone. You can break bondages and receive blessings. Specifically written for women who are impacted by passive-aggressive men, this companion book to **Standing Victoriously in the Battle** and **Weapons to Stand Boldly and Win the Battle**, gives you specific tools to use today and throughout the journey to healthful living.

Take the risk to move from victim to victorious by:
- Pondering the process questions in the book
- Applying the key thoughts
- Journaling your newfound insights
- Reviewing the chapters frequently and implementing the equipping tools
- Allowing the Holy Spirit to heal your wounded heart
- Living transformed lives, by being proactive and intentional
- **Practice, Practice and Practice!**

*"**Timely!** This dynamic book is needed to expose the riveting affects of a silent killer – passive aggression.*
~ **Pastor Neshella Mitchell, The Glory House Fellowship Church**

*"**Hallelujah!** This book gives keen insight and clear understanding of God's design for setting the captives free. Issues of crisis, trauma and drama brought on by passive-aggressive cycles are addressed with clarity and compassion. This book is like a roadmap to help readers avoid the pitfalls and move from pity to prayer and praise."*
~ **Rev. Dr. Sabrina D. Black, National Biblical Counseling Association President**

*"**Insightful!** I strongly urge you to thoroughly read this book and allow the Lord to change your life and the lives of those you love. The Christian community has been waiting for someone to write about the confusion and pain that passive aggression brings into families. This enlightening book shows you can be free of the trap that keeps you from enjoying the best God has for you. Your life can be full of joy and contentment, and this book points the way."*
~ **Betsey Hayford, Co-Senior Pastor, Eastside Foursquare Church**

*"**Invaluable!** In my thirty plus years providing therapy, I have not seen such a practical and insightful book that speaks directly to passive-aggressive relationships."*
~ **Rosalia Cardenas McDonnell MA, LMHC**

Contents

Foreword

"Those who live in the shelter of the Most High, will find rest in the shadow of the Almighty. He alone is my refuge, my place of safety; he is my God, and I trust him." (Psalm 91:1-2)

Hallelujah and High Praise for this book, *Breaking Passive-Aggressive Cycles - The Silent Cry of Christian Women*. The author, Dee Brown shows keen insight into the scriptures and a clear understanding of God's design for setting the captives free. She speaks with compassion and a heart of sincere sorrow at the statistics of today's broken relationships and marriages which are not what God intended for them to be. She has been there and the Lord has comforted her and equipped her to comfort others. This backdrop against the pain of reality when love doesn't last and when leaving doesn't lead to cleaving, creates a dynamic text filled with truth, transparency and triumph.

Dee's words are timeless and transcend cultures. People from all walks of life around the world will be impacted by *Breaking Passive-Aggressive Cycles - The Silent Cry of Christian Women*. Brown gives guidelines for the church, for counselors and for family and friends on how to respond, relate, and repair those who have been damaged by the cycle of passive-aggressive behaviors. She helps those who are single avoid poor choices and opens the way for critical dialogue. She helps those who are married see the error in their ways so that they can repent and the marriage can thrive through Jesus Christ Our Lord. You may be separated or divorced from your spouse and the life you dreamed of living, but know that nothing can separate you from the love of God and the destiny He has for your life.

The crisis, trauma and drama brought on by passive-aggressive cycles can lead to numerous emotional, physical, mental, social and spiritual maladies. Dee addresses these issues with clarity and compassion. As a survivor of much devastation she seeks to help others avoid the pitfalls and provides roadmap to help you navigate through them.

Dee, can take anyone who reads this book from PITY to PRAYER and PRAISE. She has learned how to move from the Mess to the Message; to break through the BONDAGE to BLESSINGS. No matter what has happened in your relationship. No matter who did what, why or when; Dee can help you give up GUILT for a lifetime of GRACE, as you move from being a VICTIM to living VICTORIOUSLY.

The Questions, the Power Tools, and Prayers throughout the text will encourage you to be transformed by application of the key principles. Utilizing the journaling process, Dee has recommended, will also aide you on the journey. Dear reader, be encouraged. With every NEW MORNING, there are NEW MERCIES and NEW MIRACLES. Let Dee's words help you give voice to your silent cry, so that you may experience shouts of joy.

Rev. Dr. Sabrina D. Black
Author, Counselor, International Speaker
President, National Biblical Counseling Association

Introduction

~ *Crying Out from the Chaos* ~

"The Lord is my rock, my fortress, and my savior; my God is my rock, in whom I find protection." (Psalm 18:2)

This book is written for Christian women who suffer with inner turmoil because they live with, are connected to, or function within passive-aggressive relationships. The **silent cry of women** experiencing turbulence can be heard all over the world. This is my third book on living victoriously when faced with adversity or life experiences which create spiritual warfare battles and personal struggles. The material is designed to equip those in faith-based communities to recognize and support the bondage breaking of various forms of abuse, specifically passive-aggression. It is not a pop-culture phase. Passive aggression is a set of behaviors which can, and often does, destroy relationships. Christian women have learned to **silence the cry** and mask their pain. Over time, the silence moved into a secret life, invisible to others and then to self. The truth on the following pages will assist women in unmasking the traits, tactics and tendencies of passive-aggressive people. It will also assist women in uncovering their own patterns of a "passive-aggressive dance." It is a dance, because it takes two people moving in an unhealthy circular pattern, as each person attempts to protect themselves from pain or exposure.

Women, by learning to break the silence and being honest about the relational realities, you will experience a path of living in victory, wholeness and peace. Ladies, you will also receive insight, practical tools, encouragement and empowerment in strategically breaking harmful generational patterns and cycles. While often misunderstood, the term passive-aggressive behavior becomes clear when you understand the origins, the traits, and the cyclical patterns. The enemy has maximized strategic tactics to kill the spirit, hope, peace, dreams and visions of women who live in chaotic or abusive environments. Spiritual warfare runs rampant in passive-aggressive relationships.

The birthing of this book came from being in the trenches with women for the last two decades. **I encourage you to read this material out loud.** Due to the content of this book, it is important for you to receive the truth into your own heart and spirit. Seeing, hearing, speaking and then applying the information is all part of the restorative process. **Ladies, do not try to rush through this book. You will need to pace yourself as you read the material because it is a process book.** My sisters, as you work through this book, ultimately you will gain knowledge and wisdom to expose what I call **"the web and world"** of a passive-aggressive person. Identifying passive-aggressive characteristics, learning to set healthy boundaries, stopping the generational cycles, grieving losses, and understanding spiritual battles will equip you to live victoriously in the future. It is extremely important that you learn to be celebrated and not simply tolerated. In doing so, you will need to believe and claim who you are, which is a mighty woman of valor and daughter of the Almighty God.

During the last decade my own awareness has increased as more and more clients began relating the stories of verbal and emotional abuse, or passive-aggressive invalidation. There is a rise giving way to a full epidemic of Christian women who are living with, or are connected to, passive-aggressive men. While equally devastating, there aren't enough pages to address all forms of abuse. For clarity sake, the sole emphasis of this material is to speak specifically to passive aggression in the Christian community and how the enemy, Satan, is utilizing apathy and unresponsiveness to mask this pervasive issue. Women lack the recognition and realization of the roots of these stifling passive-aggressive relationships. For many, their personal experiences run so deep, that the mouth cannot even speak about the wounds, confusion, shame, disillusionment and hurt within the heart. If there is not a place to safely share, people become immobilized to speak about the circumstances in their daily lives. This will ultimately foster isolation from others. Healing and restoring communities are essential in breaking this isolation and shame.

My sisters, your Abba Father is ready and available to walk with you, in and through the transforming and rebuilding process. **Be expectant!** The season of favor and freedom is waiting for you. In declaring God's promises and picking up the tools throughout this book, you now hold the key to walking through the transformational process. Within the chapters you will see equipping tools highlighted as **Power Tools**. *These short statements are action items for you to open your process of discovery. God has already given you the power; these tools are plugged in to His purposes specifically for your empowerment.* Declare this as a new day in your life and your Abba Father, who led you to this book, has a pathway for you to be delivered from the lifestyle that wraps you in the web and world of a passive-aggressive person.

I am passionate about seeing people set free from any barriers or bondages which prevent them from living a transparent, transformational life while fulfilling their destiny and purpose. It is my prayer that a voice will be given back to Christian women who are repetitiously stating, *"Who will hear my silent cry?"* Living with or being connected to a passive-aggressive person is a persistent struggle. The days of downplaying the daily frustrations and living with constant urgency and turmoil are at a critical crossroads. The subject of passive aggression and abuse must not be taken lightly, because it suppresses the destructive truth for people in faith-based communities. The spiritual battle for women will be the tendency to avoid breaking the silence of passive aggression and intentionally pursuing healing.

Ladies, the Lord has heard your cry and has set in motion a passageway for your relief, deliverance and freedom. The Abba Father wants all those who are oppressed, depressed and suppressed to be liberated; walk in security, live in safety, experience significance and receive love. He does not want you to live in a state of confusion, chaos, discontentment or despair. Nor does He want you to tolerate being devalued through abuse. When the Lord came, He had a mission which He shared in the following passage:

~ Prayer ~

"The spirit of the Sovereign Lord is upon me, for the Lord has anointed me to bring good news to the poor. He has sent me to comfort the brokenhearted and to proclaim that captives will be released and prisoners will be freed. He has sent me to tell those who mourn that the time of the Lord's favor has come . . . to all who mourn . . .he will give a crown of beauty for ashes, a joyous blessing instead of mourning, festive praise instead of despair." (Isaiah 61:1-3)

~ VALIDATION ~

"The Lord is my rock, my fortress, and my savior; My God is my rock in who I find protection."
(Psalm 18:2)

Chapter 1

Personal Crisis of Confidence ~
Defining Abuses and Passive Aggression

"Praise the Lord! For He has heard my cry for mercy! The Lord is my strength and shield. I trust Him with all my heart. He helps me, and my heart is filled with joy. I burst out in songs of thanksgiving." (Psalm 28:6-7)

I am very excited you picked up this book. It is not an accident. This book focuses on the relationships and fallout of passive-aggressive behaviors, specifically within faith-based communities. There are many books available addressing abuse. Therefore, in this chapter, I will give only basic definitions of abuse in order to set a foundation, particularly concentrating on passive aggression from a Christ-centered perspective. However, now it is time to expose the madness of a subversive and insidious epidemic within the Christian community. Sisters, it is time to step out of a fog and tear down the veil of deception.

The book is written to give voice for those who are repetitiously stating, *"Who will hear my silent cry?"* I will also describe the tactics of the enemy of our souls and how he has infiltrated faith-based communities to bring disruption, disunity and relational hostility. Passive aggression can manifest itself in roles from the bishop, to the pastor, to the man in the pew. When the behavior takes hold, the role provides no immunity. James 1:5 states, *"If you need wisdom, asks our generous Abba Father, and He will give it to you. . ."* I pray this book will provide a practical guide to understand passive aggression. So now the question is, how did we get this term passive aggression and what does it mean?

The phrase, passive aggression, was originally coined by the military to describe soldiers who exhibited a mixture of passive resistance and argumentative compliance. This behavior was in response to the strict, controlled, compliant and mandatory environment of the military. The soldiers fought losing their identity and being forced to conform to other peoples' expectations, while not getting their needs met or acknowledged. Periodically, soldiers were found dodging responsibilities. However, it wasn't openly defiant behavior because that would have come with a personal cost. In some cases severe consequences would ensue to control the defiant behavioral patterns. Since, the word originates in the military; it is naturally a word of battle. The passive- aggressive person believes that people may step on them, so their main strategy is resistance.

Living with, or being connected to a passive-aggressive man not only creates a sense of shame but also a crisis in personal confidence. A woman may be a very competent, influential and effective person in other areas of life, yet, when hit with the subversive passive-aggressive behavior, many women say they feel like a powerless child. Women then tend to respond to this emotion by striving harder, all the while, veiling the truth and pain of their reality. My sisters, I realize you are constantly attempting to manage internal turmoil and chaos. However, crisis management only fosters more pandemonium in a passive-aggressive environment. Over time, women will suffer and become physically, emotionally and spiritually sick under the duress and stress of an oppressive environment. The internal chaos rings of indescribable messages about what you feel, yet can't explain.

Confusion swirls in the mind over mixed messages and distorted communication styles of a passive-aggressive person. When this occurs, you begin to question your own ability to communicate, as thoughts, such as, **"I know I said _____. Why does he keep denying what I said? Maybe I didn't really say_____."** Second guessing your thinking and circumstances is part of the internal self talk associated with passive-aggressive relationships. In the confusion, you begin trying to make sense of inexpressible incidences, because you can't quite pinpoint the subtle patterns. Yet, a myriad of emotions twirl around in your head with no place to land. It makes no sense, yet it is the reality of your surroundings and you may not even know why. As a consequence of not being able to identify the cyclical patterns, these passive-aggressive relationships are allowed to prevail and spiral out of control, before the truth begins to surface.

*Take Note: *"It is my hope that you will be equipped, as you continue to read and implement the tools addressed in this book. This may be a good time to take your journal and begin the process of jotting down insights. As you record the insights, you will be building a toolkit to use going forward."*

By nature the passive-aggressive personality erupts in a hidden form of emotional abuse and invalidation that deteriorates, devastates and demolishes relationships. A passive-aggressive individual has an uncanny ability to give the impression that you are the cause of any relational unrest. Whether spiritual, emotional, verbal, physical, sexual, or passive aggression, abuses are real human issues which must be addressed in society, and especially within faith-based communities. As churches deafen to the cries of women, apathy expands and serves to perpetuate the destructive impact of various forms of abuse. If allowed, the process destroys families and weakens churches, society and ultimately nations. I pray leaders will see the necessity of becoming involved in hearing the cries of these women. It is essential they identify behaviors that lead people away from the healthy relationships the Lord intended.

As passive-aggressive patterns surface, women may see relational aspects that have burdened them with a husband, a pastor, a boss, boyfriend, brother or a father. While this book is written specifically for women, the information is genderless. I have known and worked with women who also exhibited passive-aggressive patterns, behaviors and tendencies which greatly impacted men. Yet, as a rule, men do not have to survive with the type of fear women deal with when connected to hostile men. For the most part, when women exhibit passive aggression it is usually due to the:

- Result of having been sexually abused. These women make an internal vow which says, "I will never allow myself to be that powerless again." So they deal with any real or perceived emotional or relational threat with aggressive behavioral patterns, instead of learning to become assertive about getting their needs met.
- Result of being betrayed by other women. Women who have been betrayed by other women are deeply hurt. They make a vow which won't allow closeness or connection out of fear of further rejection. What you see is not what you get from these wounded women. Betrayed women can become defensive and hypersensitive.
- Result of growing up with perfectionist expectations from significant authority figures.
- Result of unhealed father or mother wounds.

Power Tool: *"The Abba Father and His Word gives us hope. Know that He has heard the cry of His daughter and the plans for you are good. Declare that as a child of the Living God, you know that He is near. With Him, you can march forward with confidence, clarity and boldness. Choose to proclaim that you can do all things through the Lord Jesus Christ, who has and will strengthen you. Amen."*

If you have unhealthy experiences currently and in your past, you may become triggered while reading this book. I encourage you to pay close attention to your thought patterns and responses to certain triggers. Do not run from them, but rather use these triggers to serve as information for your healing pathway. *The triggers are a strategic part of identifying areas you need to acknowledge, and heal from, in order to walk triumphantly and in liberty.* A journal is a useful tool for: 1) doing personal process while recording your insights 2) releasing emotions you may want to communicate to the Lord, and 3) reviewing and doing self-examination. In addition, journals pinpoint milestones of growth, as well as expose areas that need to be addressed as you move forward. After journaling, I encourage you to read these insights out loud. Many times the Holy Spirit will enable you to uncover veiled truths as you hear yourself speak them. Frequently, the Holy Spirit will expose hidden characteristics of passive-aggressive cycles in your relationships. The clarity and information you receive will assist you in unpacking any emotional baggage.

There is a path which leads to serenity. There is anticipation, courage and strength available in, during, and after the recovery journey. Hold on, my sisters! Keep your faith ignited by fanning the flame of hope. The Lord does not want us to be imprisoned by unresolved wounds, broken hearts or un-healed damaged emotions. When we do not heal areas of hurt, shame, rejection or grieve wounding losses, the enemy feeds off these areas in an attempt to keep you in bondage. God says, *"Yes, I have loved you, my people, with an everlasting love. With unfailing love I have drawn you to myself." (Jeremiah 31:3)* I encourage you to take this scripture and personalize it by inserting your name and speaking it out loud. *Ask yourself how it makes you feel.*

It is not the Lord's plan that you experience consistent times of abuse or shame in any way from the men in your life. Putting truth into the light and dealing with passive aggression head-on, will restore women to walk towards a path of wholeness. Be encouraged while becoming empowered as you continue to read and receive tools to bring victory from suppression, oppression or depression. *Live and walk no longer in silence.* The Lord has heard your cry.

Dear Ones, keep in mind, the path to healing is a journey. The word journey means passage, crossing and voyage. That is exactly what the Lord will be walking alongside you to accomplish. The word also implies you will be passing through a process. In taking a journey you have an end destination as well. You cross from one place to get to another place. The Holy Spirit will be faithful to guide you as you take one step at a time, one day at a time. Every now and then, it may even be one second at a time. The first step may be recognizing where you are and knowing the Lord never intended you to live in daily fear.

"The Lord is my light and my salvation, so why should I be afraid? The Lord is my fortress, protecting me from danger, so why should I tremble?" (Psalm 27:1)

It's important that we briefly turn our attention towards understanding covert (hidden) and overt (obvious) forms of abuse. The steps towards healing and restoration are *awareness, acknowledgement, accountability, and taking action.* Another part of healing is taking ownership for your own responsive patterns. It is the Holy Spirit's intent that you be able to embrace the joy of living in your true and authentic self by being prepared with strategic tools. In order to be on the same page, it is essential you have a working definition of various forms of abuse and their link to passive aggression. Physically, emotionally, spiritually and verbally abusive environments involve toxic relationships. The signs of passive-aggressive relationships are more subtle and less obvious than the other forms of abuse. Yet, there are consistent cycles you will begin to see more clearly. The clarity will help you to stop the toxic impact.

~ DOMESTIC VIOLENCE ABUSE ~

"The Spirit of the Sovereign Lord is upon me, for the Lord has anointed me to bring news to the poor. He has sent me to comfort the brokenhearted and to proclaim that captives will be released and prisoners will be freed." (Isaiah 61:1-3)

Society, to date, has little difficulty acknowledging the existence of physical or sexual abuse, although, women around the world continue to suffer under the toleration of various abuses inflicted upon them. Currently, society tends to group physical harm and verbal abuse under the same heading; domestic violence. Domestically violent men deliberately intend to destroy the personhood of women and children in their lives. Domestically violent environments are thick with dehumanizing and must be dealt with immediately. The violence will get worse, so do not minimize the intent of the domestically violent person. God's Word instructs people "... *Stop your violence and oppression and do what is just and right. . .*" (*Ezekiel 45:9*) Aggression alone is not synonymous with violence. Humans have been given the God-given ability to be fighters and lovers. Aggression unrestrained and undisciplined becomes violent. At this point, I would like to communicate and encourage my sisters who are in domestic violence situations to seek help as soon as possible. Domestic violence is an overt (open and obvious) form of abuse which is rampant around the world and has flooded into the lives of those in the Christian community.

Domestic violence, or battering abuse, is a major cruel stripping assault on a person's body, confidence, value, identity, self-esteem and self-respect. The very things which the domestic violator strips from their victim are the exact same things the violator lacks. Domestic violence is an escalated level of abuse in which a person intimidates with their size, strength, or presence in order to dominate, over-power and physically hurt another individual into submission. This submissive surrender then completely strips a person of the inner ability to fight for truth and freedom. The victim is completely controlled and on the path of potentially being physically violated or even murdered. The person experiencing consistent domestic violence hushes their gut feelings and truth. The abuser has a completely distorted view of their identity. Remember, the abuse will continue to get worse over time.

Experts have identified that a domestically violent man who has a deep-seeded hatred for women is known as a *misogynist*. This comes from a Greek word, *miso*, meaning hatred and *gyne*, meaning women. ***Misogyny is gender specific and primarily the person will utilize emotional, spiritual and physical abuse to totally control women.*** The misogynist distrusts anything and everything a woman does and blows it out of proportion. They may have been abused by a female at an early age. Most of the time, misogynistic men experienced emotional or physical harm from women or a specific woman during their childhood and adolescent years. Thus, this type of man treats all women with stored up bitterness and hatred. He may date or marry, but becomes vicious and is an extremist in the hateful behaviors towards his wife or girlfriend. If a woman dares to cry, it reinforces a message of the utter weakness of women which the misogynist loathes. Tears from women are seen by this person as being threatening, and yet it often brings on a high level of rage. If you are connected to a misogynist, seek help as quickly as possible.

Power Tool: The Lords speaks strongly in Matthew 12:35-36 which states, "A good person produces good things from the treasury of a good heart, and an evil person produces evil things from the treasury of an evil heart. And I tell you this; you must give an account on judgment day for every idle word you speak. The words you say will either acquit you or condemn you."

The fundamental basis of toxic domestically violent relationships involves some level of insecurity, lack of self-control, and a thirst for controlling power. Men who are and have been domestic violence abusers now generally understand their aggression is punishable by law. However, in view of this knowledge, many of these aggressive men have become more secretive. The underground traits and tendencies may resemble passive aggression. This response has far-reaching consequences on the family, employment, community, nations and ultimately the world. Women often ask, "Where is God in the midst of this profound injustice?" God also saw His own son abused by humanity. Yet, Jesus died, paying the ultimate cost for all of humanity. In God's love for us, He has given us a free-will to choose. With that gift, came the human ability to do evil as well. The good news is, God is not idle. He hears the cries of those calling out to Him and will heal and restore your broken heart.

All those who abuse must address the root of the rage. It is my prayer that sons, grandsons and fathers will take back everything that the enemy has stolen. I pray, men will rise up, take ownership, receive restoration and help other men to stop the generational genocide. The very earth is rumbling and calling you to gather as men in community and stop the insanity of abuse. The Lord has been witness to the devastation of parental instability and the fatherless. He is the Heavenly Father who heals those who experience physical, emotional, relational or spiritual abandonment and abuse. Men have got to speak out in a brotherhood to help other men change their courses of madness, violence and abuse toward women. Men, do not allow the enemy of your soul to snatch any more dreams, visions, or families. Do not let the enemy destroy your destiny and identity.

"Lord, I pray the men will hear the battle-cry of abused women. I pray they will be convicted to admit the truth and get the help they need to stop abusing. I pray they acknowledge the reality of who they have become by wounding and killing the spirit and soul of women all over the world. Lord, awaken these men who have experienced the dulling and denial of owning their choices. Lord, laser beam the roots of their rage and violent thinking. Illuminate the truth. Awaken them to the deadening of their senses and the apathy which perpetuates the cyclic behaviors and in some cases death. Thank you Lord for your promises to rescue and restore us from all bondage, oppression and hardships."

Domestic violence, in any degree, is evil in the eyes of the Lord. The Word says, *"The wicked conceive evil; they are pregnant with trouble and give birth to lies. They dig a deep pit to trap others, and then fall into it themselves. The trouble they make for others backfires on them." (Psalm 7:14-16)* You were not designed to permit constant, degrading abuse to permeate your mind, heart and soul. Ask the Lord for help to be bold and consistent in setting boundaries against domestic violence. Ask Him to give you a sound mind and a discerning spirit to know when, and how, to step out of a violent situation. Ask the Lord to send others around you who are willing to walk with you in your healing from abuse. Pray for the Lord to send people who hear your hearts cry and believe your story.

Domestic abusers are weak in personal character and yet attempt to weaken others so they can feel a sense of personal dominance. Regardless of a person's socio-economic status or position, domestic violence occurs. It is a tragic worldwide epidemic and it is time to stop the toleration of abuses in society and especially in faith-based communities. Ladies, violence should not be tolerated, or hidden under the veil of "blind submission." As Christian women, we open our hearts and yield to the Sovereignty of the Lord. The Holy Spirit guides us in loving one another. This does not mean we are to connect with each other through fearful acquiescence. **Many women in faith-based communities remain silent, thinking they have failed or let God down. Others believe they do not deserve to be valued or even to live**. God tells His people in Ezekiel 45:9 to "*Stop your violence and oppression and do what is just and right.*" Dear Ones, break the stillness of the voice echoing in your head telling you not to share your reality with others. I encourage you to speak with someone you can trust.

The Lord takes violence and abuse in any form very seriously. Abuse is a violent sin which God abhors. When we look into the Bible we get God's definition of the word violence. In the Old Testament the word "*chamac*" means to be violent. It also describes violence as being sadistic, vicious, brutal, hateful, evil, criminal, aggressive, merciless, and terror-making. It also implies an intentional mistreatment of others in malicious ways. In our legal system, physical abuse within the home, relationships or family is called domestic violence.

A domestically violent person is a controller who intentionally hurts people. If a domestic abuser pulls your hair, shoves you, breaks personal items, twists your arm, sexually abuses you, drives too fast, throws things, curses, or hits you, even once, get out of that relationship. Take these signs seriously. Remember, you have a divine right to leave a domestically abusive relationship, when distinctly appropriate. "*The prudent see danger and take precautions. The uncertain go blindly on and suffer the consequences.*" *(Proverbs 27:12)* It is not easy to step away from a domestically abusive relationship. If you need to seek help, I implore you to do so promptly! (*Refer to the back of this book for an action plan*). Domestic violence does not get better without intervention.

One of my clients stated; "*Having been raised in an aggressive environment, she thought her abuser kept things confusing and unclear. Although, she knew in her heart of hearts something was not right. She felt the manipulation by the pull of aggressive behavior and what had been explained to her as love. She shared this mixed messaging was very confusing. She could not see the reality of the abuse until she was out from under the abuser's control.*"

Many times, Christian women who are connected to abusive men struggle with the tension of walking a Christ-centered life and the masked life of a violent relationship. So many times, women do not tell even safe people about the struggle because they hope to protect the image of their family, children or even the reputation of the abusive spouse. Frequently, these women are shamed and don't feel they can tell anyone. This seems to be especially true within faith-based communities, which should be a safe place to expose and receive support against abuses. Sadly, I have heard time and time again, from women for whom this has not been the case. Most faith-based communities do not speak about abuse from the pulpit or encourage women to seek refuge and protection. However, Psalm 138:8 says, "*The Lord will work out His plans for my life; for your faithful love, O Lord, endures forever. . .*" Dear Ones, the Lord will lead and strengthen you to walk in victory with new perspectives and wisdom. Breaking the silence of abuse may release some fears. However, as you read the following words reflect and become strengthened.

"*So you have not received a spirit that makes you fearful slaves, instead, you received God's Spirit when He adopted you as His own children. Now we call Him, Abba Father. For His Spirit joins with our spirit to affirm that we are God's children (daughters). And since we are His children, we are heirs. In fact, together with Christ we are heirs of His glory.*" (*Romans 8:15-16*)

VERBAL ABUSE ~ WORDS WOUND

"All day long you plot destruction. Your tongue cuts like a sharp razor; you're an expert at telling lies."(Psalm 52:2)

Verbal abuse is a destructive form of overt emotional abuse. It is the systematic use of harmful words or sharp tone of voice in an attempt to manage and control another person. All forms of abuse are toxic, and will eventually involve some form of verbal and emotional maltreatment. Whenever a person is connected in toxic relationships it can be very draining, shaming, emotionally painful, and may trigger anger. You feel miserable, frustrated, and at times, powerless. People who verbally abuse, lack compassion and feel justified in the ill-treatment of others. It is important to discern if you are in a toxic relationship since it can be destructive to your mind, body and soul. You cannot heal what you do not name or understand.

Ask yourself the following general questions to determine if you are in a toxic relationship:

- Do you feel lifted-up, or torn-down when in the presence of particular people?
- Do you feel you have been robbed of your sense of dignity?
- Do you get fearful and seemingly walk on eggshells when in a certain person's presence?
- Do you feel like your stress level soars when engaging with a toxic person?
- Do you feel better, or worse, after being around them for any length of time?
- Do you get physical symptoms after being in their company?
- Do you dread going to home, work or family events?
- Do you feel relationally and emotionally safe around this person?
- Do you feel their words convey love, irritation or rage?

It is important to recognize that toxic people have issues and yet, they do not take responsibility for their actions. Nor do they seek help to grow and stop their specific harmful patterns. That does not mean you are to continue enabling toxic patterns and cycles. Recognition is one of the foundational steps towards your healing journey. At this moment in life, you may feel like you're losing it in the presence of a toxic person. The patterns of toxic people can *engulf* you over a period of time. It is not part of the Lord's desire for you to be abused, accused or misused. Now that you have determined if you are in a toxic relationship, you are ready to take the next action steps. My sisters, keep on reading!

God has a lot to say about all forms of abuse. The Hebrew word for verbal abuse is; "*gadaph.*" The root definition of this word means to cut or wound. Ephesians 4:29 gives us a view into what the Lord thinks about verbal abuse. The scripture says. "*Don't use foul or abusive language. Let everything you say be good and helpful, so that your words will be an encouragement to those who hear them.*" Verbal abuse, like emotional abuse is usually rationalized by the victim, as well as the abuser. Verbal abusers use words or harsh tones of voice to control. Verbal abuse is intended to destroy a person's self-worth by devaluing, humiliating and slandering. Many of the behaviors of abusers are also the traits of the Enemy-of-Our-Souls. Our enemy did not design abuse; however, he will try to capitalize on our life situations. One of the names in the Bible for the enemy is "*Slanderer*". The Slanderer will attempt to cause people to doubt their identity. Abuse strips people of their true identity.

People who verbally assault will intimidate with constant threatening, shaming, accusing, belittling, name-calling and poignant insulting if you do not comply with their requests; all to create a one up-one down way of relating. If you read Ephesians 4:31, the Lords elaborates on verbal wounding and cutting. The verse tells us to "*Get rid of all bitterness, rage, harmful anger, harsh words, slander, as well as all types of evil behavior.*" Verbal and emotional abuses leave painful scars on a person's heart and soul. Yes, at times we all become angry and raise our voices when involved in the heat of an argument. It is entirely different when the destructive patterns of verbal shame are unleashed on a **day-to-day basis** and **escalated in intensity** over the course of time.

Although this list is not all-inclusive, people who are verbally abusive exhibit any, or all, of the following characteristics:

- **Blames** others for their own uncontrolled anger, failures, rage, mistakes or bad moods. For example: *"If you weren't so lazy, I wouldn't have to keep reminding you to do things and then I wouldn't get so upset."*
- **Denial** is used by not admitting or taking responsibility for personal actions or words, but accusations are directed at others. It is a protective and coping mask that allows a person to deal with real or perceived threats or inner turmoil. For example: *"Where did you get that insane idea? I know you think you told me, but you never did. You can't get anything straight!"*
- **Distorting or Discrediting** is a method to deny situations, abilities or skills of others and is done by twisting facts or even making them up. For example: *"You can't sing! Why did you think it would sound any different? You wouldn't know good singing if you heard it."*
- **Manipulation** is done by appealing to, or using, another person's sense of responsibility in order to obtain personal gain. Manipulation undermines a person's confidence in order to control them. For example: *"If you really cared about me, you would do this for me."*
- **Sarcasm/Teasing/Name-calling or Humiliating** is all done at the emotional expense of another person. Verbally abusive statements include ridicule, shame and embarrassment. For example: *"She will never become anything worthwhile because she is not smart enough." "You have to excuse her, because she doesn't know any better." "I should have known it was a women driver." "I was only teasing you!"*

~ Can you relate to any of the above statements? If so, then it is time to take action! ~

* **Power Tool**: *"Ladies, if verbal abuse escalates to physical abuse, search for help immediately. You must protect yourself. If you have children, safety is especially important. You do not need to battle alone."*

EMOTIONAL ABUSE ~ BROKEN HEARTS and BROKEN SPIRIT

"The Lord is close to the brokenhearted; he rescues those whose spirits are crushed." (Psalm 34:18)

Emotional abuse is extensive in our culture, and faith-based communities are no exception. **In general, emotional abuse is a nonphysical behavior or attitude that controls, demeans, punishes or isolates a person. It is a way of relating and interacting with others to get personal desires met.** Inherent in emotionally abusive people is a repetitive cycle of manipulating, controlling and dominating tactics, so they get the outcomes they desire. They use these behaviors to maintain a position of power without considering how it affects other people. Overt (open and blatant) abuse may also include verbal, physical or sexual if it is forced upon a person without their consent. Abuse puts a person into darkness, but the light must shine. It is time to be equipped and to step out of the bondage of abuse.

Women in faith-based communities find it hard to believe their gut feelings that some people are abusive and manipulative. Women are susceptible to being emotionally blackmailed because they have a tendency to place other's wishes and feelings ahead of their own. For instance: Let's say you have a friend named Malika. Every time you refuse to comply with her requests, she will pout, withdraw or distance herself. Then you decide to ask her what is wrong. Sighing, Malika would consistently respond with, "Oh nothing." Most of the time, you resent the manipulation but you finally give-in to break the silent treatment. If you do not confront as soon as possible, Malika will continue giving you the "cold shoulder" whenever she is displeased with you. It is important to use the tool of confronting this cyclic pattern of manipulative behavior or it will inevitably continue. Ladies, not only will it continue, it will escalate and happen more often. Also, once you start compromising with one person, you will have a tendency to have the same response every time you connect with similar personalities.

Frequently, Christian women feel they are making the right biblical choice by staying in abusive relationships. Furthermore, Christian women hesitate to stand their ground or appear negative in confronting abusive realities. In an attempt to give the *benefit of a doubt*, they will incorrectly access harmful behavior by minimizing, excusing or rationalizing. Therefore, women do not address harmful patterns appropriately or in a timely manner. This type of belief permits subtle emotional abuse to be denied, by blaming self and trying even harder to make the person happy. This pattern will transcend home and continue into the work force, families and friendships.

It is important to distinguish between emotional hurt and emotional abuse. Emotional hurt and emotional abuses are very different in how they impact a person. I am sure at some point in life you have been emotionally hurt by someone. I know I have. How can you tell the difference? The following example might shed some light in distinguishing the two concepts; a boyfriend complains that he doesn't like the way you fixed dinner. Expressing that statement is not necessarily being emotionally abusive, even though the person on the other end of the comment may feel emotionally hurt. However, if the boyfriend consistently tells his girlfriend she is awful, thoughtless, selfish and totally inconsiderate for not fixing food the way he thinks it should be prepared, then he is being verbally and emotionally abusive.

In emotionally abusive relationships there is a determined intent to formulate statements or actions which leave a person feeling awful, humiliated or shamed. Additionally, this strategic undermining is ultimately done to strip the person of identity and self-worth, in order to control their actions. The girlfriend, who is trapped in that cycle, will begin an unhealthy pattern of trying harder and harder to please the boyfriend. Eventually, she will give more and more of herself away trying to *"keep the peace."* She soon discovers that specific protective measures just do not work. One day she wakes-up and doesn't know how the relationship got to a place of *"eggshell walking."* Eggshell walking is exhausting and robs you of being your authentic self. After a period of time, the outcome is physical, emotional and spiritual symptoms which eventually take their toll.

Living with or being connected to emotionally abusive people prevent you from relaxing when in their presence. Frequently, *"eggshell walking"* will have an element of fear involved. If you find yourself *"eggshell walking"* it means you have been *monitoring your words, beating around the bush or softening your phases.* Ladies, no place in scripture does the Lord support any kind of abuse. Our Abba Father has designed us as unique individuals. We are to be ourselves and speak the truth in relationships. When you walk on eggshells, you are not functioning the way you were designed and you are not being true to yourself.

Women ultimately lose all sense of personhood in the process of denying, relinquishing, rationalizing, compromising and excusing abusive behaviors. If women do not set healthy boundaries appropriately, despite the fact there are fears, they unknowingly give men the false permission to mistreat them. I want to stress a couple of fundamental truths. First, men who abuse have a personal choice, and secondly, you are not responsible for that man's abusive actions. Sisters, break the silence, declare and believe you can break this cycle when you choose to come off the roller-coaster madness!

In the process of walking towards wholeness, people come to believe that the Holy Spirit is greater than them and He has the power to restore their sanity. Coming to believe implies you will journey through a restorative process. Ladies, belief systems are built on the outcome of our life experiences. We need wisdom, truth and discernment to truly walk the process. When we firmly believe it is time for a change, we take action. We are to realistically assess what is working in our belief systems and what is not. Ladies, as you hear the voice of the Holy Spirit, you will receive wisdom.

When we honestly admit and identify our strengths and weakness, then we are on the road to sanity and wholeness. Pray that the Holy Spirit will guide you in boldly carrying out the healing process. There are three words which are significant when breaking these twisted abusive relationships. Throughout the reading of this book, I encourage you to journal your prayers and record the Holy Spirit's response to you. **One of the ways which will help you focus is by recording the following components in your journal writing**:

- **Enlightenment**: Pray the Holy Spirit will reveal all truth as you uncover tools in unveiling passive-aggressive cycles in your relationships. Ask Him to illuminate any distortions or beliefs which keep you stuck in abusive relationships. The word to *illuminate* means to shed light on, clarify, explain, or enlighten. Enlightenment will empower you to come out of any darkness. Breaking free from the chaotic behavioral cycles of passive aggression will impact the next generations.
- **Restoration**: Pray for personal healing and internal peace as you enter into the restorative process. Ask the Holy Spirit to reinstate, rebuild and repair all broken places in your heart, mind and soul. Another meaning for the word restore is to "*smarten up.*" Ladies, you are going to smarten up, gain tools and no longer be deceived or controlled by unpredictable, and deflective abusive cycles. You will learn to recognize the traits in order to become proactive with healthy responses. You need to *shout right here*, because you will be restored as you persevere in the journey.
- **Intentionality**: Pray that the Holy Spirit will give you boldness and diligence to stay focused; remain committed; and not settle for *band aid solutions* or *quick fixes*. You are a participant in your own deliverance. The Lord will honor your faith, even if you feel it is only the size of a mustard seed. The Lord expects us to be involved in the process. Being intentional will require you to be *honest* with yourself and truthful with others. This is especially true in passive-aggressive relationships, which are

two-way, cyclical connections. You must recognize your own merry-go-round patterns and come out of the passive-aggressive dance. You cannot change other people; however, you absolutely have control over how you respond to harmful, hurtful or destructive behavioral patterns. Amen!

*Power Tool: *"After you have written during your journaling times, then plan to activate the tools you receive throughout this book. In order to break the bondage and destructive patterns of passive aggression you must break any denial or rescuing behaviors."*

People do not simply arrive overnight at a place where they are in abusive relationships. So it is going to be a challenge to walk into liberty. Let's look further into some reality of the journey. You will be left with scars from the process to wholeness. However, start where you are and take the steps to proactively and purposely deal with any abuse, and oppression in your life. *It will be important to journal what works and what does not.* Stay alert and you will win the race. You must believe you can do the work to heal. Stop right here ladies, and speak life to yourself by saying out loud, *"I am worth it!"* The prophet Isaiah pours out a promise for us: *"Those who trust in the Lord will find new strength. They will soar high on wings like eagles. They will run and not grow weary. They will walk and not faint."(Isaiah 40:31)* Learning to recognize characteristics of various forms of abuse, or invalidation, will be a paramount first step. *Remember to take one day at a time and be consistent*!

Once women understand the origins, or root issues, of abusive characteristics, then they can take those truths and walk in boldness with all the authority bestowed on them from the Lord. The Holy Spirit will strengthen you to stay focused and remain knowledgeable in healing the pain of the past. Subsequently, you will be prepared to let go and move on in your life. Psalm 37:5-6 tells us to *"Commit everything you do to the Lord. Trust Him, and He will help you. He will make your innocence radiate like the dawn, and the justice of your cause will shine like the noonday sun."*

*Power Tool: *"If you have a child who you suspect may be exhibiting passive-aggressive behaviors, there are two disorders which may need to be evaluated. First, you may seek a professional to review a diagnosis for Oppositional Defiant Disorder. Secondly, Attention Deficit Disorder or Attention Deficit Hyperactivity Disorder is also possible. Both of these disorders are frequently masked as passive aggression."*

~ *Prayer* ~

"Lord, Listen to my prayer for mercy, as I cry out to you for help, as I lift my hand towards your Holy sanctuary." (Psalm 28:2)

Chapter 2

Overt and Covert Emotional Abuse ~
Invalidators

"Let all that I am wait quietly before the Lord,
for my hope is in Him." (Psalm 62:5)

When it comes to identifying the root causes and impact of emotional abuse, it is clearly not understood, or discussed, in general society or even within the Christian community. Passive aggression is often lumped in the domestic violence arena. However, it needs to be separated from domestic violence and dealt with on its own. Passive aggression can be just as destructive and devastating as domestic violent abuse. Needless to say, abuses come in various forms. The most visible form is physical abuse because people can see the outward scarring and bruising. Some women attest to the fact that the wounds of passive aggression are worse because the outcomes are rarely seen. The injuries and scars are felt internally. These internal wounds are the direct result of emotional abuses. However, it is important to understand what makes emotional hurt or rejection different from emotional abuse.

There are a few distinctions which must be understood when dealing with emotional abuse. So, the question to be answered is; how do the traits and characteristics of emotional abuse relate to passive aggression? **There are basically two main forms of emotional**

abuse. One form is called overt and the other is covert. Both forms of emotional abuse have a clear-cut element of manipulation and denial. The damage and invisible scars of emotional abuse are very difficult to heal, because memories are imprinted on our minds and hearts and it takes time to be restored. Imprints of past traumas do not mean a person cannot change their future beliefs and behaviors. As people, we do not easily forget. However, as we heal, grieve, and let go, we become clear-minded and focused to live restored and emotionally healthy.

Emotional abusers know that their significant others love or care for them. They strategically use or manipulate this emotional connection for abusive purposes. Emotional abuse is very difficult to unwrap, and discuss. One of the truths which perpetuate this is because people seldom take women who are being impacted seriously. As long as we are silent in the faith-based communities, the enemy will have an inroad to keep affecting relationships and families.

Overt (obvious, open and unconcealed) emotional abuse is an open, deliberate, constant, and destructive set of negative behaviors. These behaviors are used in an attempt to intentionally devalue, render powerless, crush, strip, control, or hurt another person. There is an overall sense the overt abuser disdains you, versus simply does not like something specifically you may be doing to irritate them. Overt emotional abuse is blatant ill-treatment which exploits others to meet a person's unmet needs. The goal of an overt abuser is victimization without regret, pretentiousness or any attempt to conceal the motive. **Overt emotional abuse frequently has an expected and predictable pattern, which escalates over time and can become physically abusive**. Emotional invalidation goes beyond rejection. It implies that your emotions are disapproved of and there is something fundamentally abnormal about you. Emotional invalidation is one of the most lethal forms of emotional abuse. It kills confidence, creativity and ultimately a person's core identity.

I am sure you know, or have met, someone who tries to make you feel as small as a bread crumb. After getting emotionally or verbally hit by this person you walked away from the experience wondering, "What in the world just happened?"After being stunned by the connection you may have felt angry and hurt. It is common to have felt shut down or dismissed in some manner. Yet, you could not quite pinpoint the reason behind the way this encounter went down.

The overt emotional abuser consistently uses tactics to throw a person off balance, which undermines self-respect, robs security, and steals a sense of worth. Ultimately, emotional abuse destroys all shred of personal identity and denying our God-given uniqueness. This is frequently accompanied by neglect, apathy, threats, indifference and violent patterns of behavior. Blatant overt attacks are premeditated to cut at the core of a person's value. Overt abuse burns a hole in the heart, leaving the residue of deep wounds and scars. The abuser also uses methods of a controlled continual sea of hurled put-downs and dishonoring statements.

Women who have experienced systematic emotional abuse lose their self-confidence and significance, diminishing the victim's ability to trust their own perceptions. Many times, Christian overt abusers utilize degrading behaviors by intimidating and controlling with scripture, all under the disguise they are "teaching or reinforcing some truth." The real truth is they are seeking control or blind conformity. It is time to throw off the shackles of past hurts, rejection and emotional betrayal.

*Take Note: The reality of the Kingdom is: *"The faithful love of the Lord never ends! His mercies never cease. Great is His faithfulness; His mercies begin afresh each morning." (Lamentations 3:22-23)* Nothing is beyond the Lord's ability to redeem. *Amen!*

SILENCED NO MORE ~ IT IS NOT GOLDEN

Let's move on to defining a form of covert emotional abuse known as passive aggression. Since passive aggression is covert, meaning hidden, subtle, deceptive, veiled, underground or secretive, it can remain unidentified for years. Passive-aggressive behaviors are real and have been ingrained in a person's personality, as an emotional and relational survival mechanism. Many times, the behavior may be exhibited through stubbornness, pettiness, arrogance and dishonesty. Passive-aggressors basically use emotional rejection, or invalidation of others to mask their personal insecurities, anger and fears. They lack the ability to openly or directly express emotions. People often get abused by others because they fail to spot their covert aggressive intentions and behaviors until after they've already been victimized. Passive aggression is hostility manifested through passivity, under the veil of masked compliance. Underneath the masked compliance are seeds of opposition and resentment.

Passive aggression can be seen in the workplace, marital relationships, churches and families. Whenever you are connected to passive-aggressive individuals, without identifying what is happening, it can be crazy-making. You feel diminished, dismissed, shut down and ignored. However, this is occurring in such a subtle way that you don't realize how to process and respond. In reality, your judging abilities are being slowly impaired by this consistent negative environment. Regardless of whether you are accommodating, pleasant, and patient, the relational situation does not improve. Then, at some point, you explode in utter frustration and despair. You suddenly find yourself screaming, slamming doors and feeling out of control yourself. You recognize you are changing into a negative person, which was not part of your identity in the past. Over time, this becomes a vicious cycle and you have begun *"the passive-aggressive dance."*

The passive-aggressive person needs to have another person "waltz" with them to make it all work. In other words, the other person becomes the target of their hostility. Often times, when passive-aggressors expresses opinions, they are consumed with worry, questioning what people think of them. Some passive-aggressive people agree with others to avoid rocking the boat or to prevent being exposed. The fear of exposing their insecurities is paramount. This is why they put on various hiding masks, which serve as protective mechanisms. It is a mode to avoid forming and fulfilling deep relational bonds, due to fear of intimacy and vulnerability. In order to re-establish your integrity, identity and self-respect, a person must have an understanding of what is happening and why.

The passive-aggressive person never learned to be in a mature and healthy relationship. Therefore, they are repeating unresolved childhood pain and bringing it all into their present relationships, at home, work or church. My sisters, there are a few things which you must know up-front to get a jumpstart of unveiling the traits and tendencies of passive aggression.

One of the main truths about passive-aggressive behavior is that it cannot be dealt with until you first uncover and identify the toxic interactions. The mind that needs to examine and assess the patterns is yours. It will be difficult, because if you have been connected to a passive-aggressive person for a long period of time, your mind has been inundated with mixed messages. The mixed messages swing from you dealing with a rational person to one who is emotionally irrational. This swinging pendulum becomes a contradiction and, therefore, a challenge. It will leave you in a paradox of inconsistency and internal conflict.

- **First, the passive-aggressive person tends to vacillate between hostile resistance towards authority figures and asking forgiveness**. At other times, making promises to change their behavioral patterns in an attempt to appease their perceived oppressor. Their behavior can show its head with or without aggravation or provocation. It is important to understand that confusion, uncertainty, upheaval and emotional chaos are indicators that you are in the presence of a passive-aggressive person.

- **Secondly, the roots of passive-aggressors cycles are not related to you**. Ladies, you don't have to try to become a diva, a beauty queen, a successful manager or a bombshell to make this person happy. It has nothing to do with what you can offer the passive-aggressive person. No, my sisters, whoever you are, the passive-aggressive is likely relating to the image of what an intimate or significant relationship means to them. They will react to anyone who threatens to enter into their private world. The person fears relational closeness and yielding to emotional compromise in any fashion.

- **Finally, one of the truths about passive-aggressive people who have come out of toxic family systems is the tendency to deny, minimize, project blame, or intellectualize**. When people minimize, they acknowledge there is a problem, but make light of the issue. Intellectualizing is an attempt to explain the problem, believing that by offering some kind of explanation, the problems will go away. This is why a passive-aggressive person can create chaos, and then go about their business as if nothing happened. Projection is about blaming the problem on others. The hope in using projection is to deflect the intensity of feelings, in order to regain a sense of security.

***Power Tool**: *"These three truths are a starting point which will help you regain your sanity as you navigate the "web and world" of passive aggression. It will help you know where you are when confusion hits. Awareness, knowledge and wisdom heal the wounded heart. When you know what is happening inside of you, then you can be more proactive."*

The passive-aggressive person is seen as being very nice most of the time. But then, all of a sudden a tornado rolls in and you are caught off guard. Let's take a look at two simple examples.

- One day a passive-aggressive husband promises to help you redo the laundry room. Time passes and nothing has been accomplished towards the completion of finishing off the laundry room. When you remind him, he gets angry and states that he never promised he was going to do any such thing. You are stunned by the inappropriate response. You have mixed feelings of hurt, confusion and guilt that he gets upset. Other times, the passive-aggressive behavior will show up in a more subtle way.

- A person recalls the day her best friend committed to supporting her in sticking to a fitness program. They agreed to meet certain days of the week to exercise. She began to lose more weight than the friend. Her friend starts missing the days they worked-out together. Then her birthday rolls around and the friend gives her a box of candy. Sugarcoated hostility is an identifying behavior of passive-aggressive people.

Some women have related experiencing passive-aggression at their workplace. The organization you work for is known for being a good place to work due to the perks and pay. From all outward appearances, people seem polite and friendly. However, under the surface of the organization is a controlled culture. There are unspoken rules which prevent people from speaking out at company meetings. Although the company proclaims they make decisions with the input of their employees, but very rarely does the feedback become implemented. They also state they want everyone to feel free to speak up, claiming an open door policy. Yet, whenever anyone does speak out, the leaders thank them and then ignore the input. Communication is indirect, frequently leaving employees guessing at what is acceptable behavior. The main unspoken rule is, **"Don't rock the boat."**

Passive-aggressive patterns can be seen in your family, friends, partner, or co-worker. Someone who says they respect, admire or love you, yet, their actions send you a message of irritation, opposition and antagonism, you will definitely deal with confusion. You wonder, "What did I do wrong?" Passive-aggressive people throw snowballs with hard rocks inside. One of the best things you can learn is to recognize and respond in ways which prevent destructive cycles. If someone screams and hits you, or threatens to kill you, then you know you've been abused. It is not so easy when you are being impacted by veiled or subtle actions, which on the surface appear to be caring. It is hard to obtain tangible evidence to validate your feelings when coping with covert emotional abuse.

It is important to recognize the passive-aggressive person has buried their painful or negative emotions alive, developing a survival mechanism which I call **frozen emotions**. *Frozen emotions are those stifled feelings which were not dealt with at the time of the original event or trauma.* This protective mechanism will eventually cause a battle within, which is manifested outwardly as passive-aggression. Negative emotions which were repressed on a regular basis in emotionally unsafe environments will erupt sooner or later. These eruptions are part of the passive-aggressive person's main operation, which can surface through silent periods of blame and moodiness. Therefore, unresolved hurt, shame, anger, fear, rejection or feelings of abandonment go underground. Frozen emotions tend to pop up whenever the person is triggered or feels emotionally threatened.

It is not uncommon for the passive-aggressive person to exhibit certain behaviors whenever they are triggered by emotional hurt or feelings of rejection. Passive-aggressive behaviors are an attempt to defend self from further, real or perceived, pain. At that point a person will simply react rather than consider healthy responses. The ramification of dealing with the consistent frustration of passive aggression eventually affects a person physically, emotionally and spiritually.

Passive aggression is usually a reactionary behavior to a present situation which is rooted in past negative experiences. Thus, when a situation comes up which feels the same way, it can trigger old feelings. **A trigger takes a person back to previous life events and resurrects the same emotional response**. The way a person perceives, and gives meaning, to those negative experiences is often more powerful than the original event. Passive-aggressive men, who are walking a restorative process, have told me, after being triggered, there are some specific thoughts which run through their minds. These internal voices of self-deception have a common thread at the very core of the message. These thoughts come forward when they sense a potential threat, injustice or personal exposure. The men I have coached to break passive-aggressive patterns, call this type of inner turmoil, "the war within."

Internal Voices ~ The War Within

- I must protect myself from being exposed. If necessary, lie when needed.
- I must not allow others to see any of my insecurities.
- I must find a way to control the situation, or the other person.
- I must shut the person down and avoid direct confrontation while preventing vulnerability.
- I must attack before being attacked.
- I must not make a mistake or admit I am wrong.
- I must not look "stupid."
- I will never "win" so why try?

Men, who are wounded and choose not to heal the roots of the above internal voices, will continue walking in self-deception. Often, believing their defensive reaction is completely justified. Most of these voices were rooted as seeds at a very young age. Then as life went on these seeds became beliefs. These beliefs turned into protective mechanisms. The protective mechanisms became the filters upon which they weigh all emotional and relational connection. In looking at the above messages you can see the root of fear, especially the fear of being exposed.

Women, who have lived with or are connected to passive aggressive men, will need to heal from the drama and trauma of the relationships. Throughout this material women will learn to heal from past pain and be able to implement healthy responses to painful triggers. Obtaining understanding and knowledge will equip women with healing tools. These tools will enable women in choosing not to let the past control their present behavior and thinking.

Some women will find it difficult to deal with the years of pain sustained in passive-aggressive relationships. If this is your situation and you feel stuck, it may be necessary to seek help, support and accountability. Otherwise resentment, anger and bitterness may produce constant inner turmoil. Choosing to turn our choices over to the Lord is not a onetime decision. At times, it is a moment-by-moment, deliberate choice. ***When you know what to do if you are experiencing an emotional hook, you can then get off the roller coaster faster and faster each time.***

Passive-aggressive (P-A) people are very skilled invalidators who are fearful of being vulnerable or exposed. Individuals with P-A behavior express anger or hostility through indirect, manipulative and passive actions. For instance, instead of saying "I don't have time to stop at the cleaners on the way to work." Some passive-aggressive people will simply not do it. If confronted as to why, they will make statements such as; *"I forgot" or "You can pick it up tomorrow. I am too tired to go back out now."* Still, other people may agree to complete the task and then not follow through to completion. If the person making the request becomes frustrated after numerous similar scenarios, the passive-aggressive one will use a tool of simply looking at them calmly and not saying a word. The look is meant to convey, **"What is your problem? Look at you raising your voice. You are the one who is angry, not me.***" I know some of you can relate!* However, if the shoe were on the other foot, they would expect that you would have gone to the cleaners. Double standards are common among passive-aggressive people. Unspoken expectations and mixed messages will trap you constantly, and are part of the *"crazy making web of passive aggression."* Ask the Holy Spirit to release:

- Insight and wisdom to make the necessary changes.
- A discerning ability to see the reality and not minimize the facts.
- Strength, courage and a willing heart to choose a healing path.
- Increased faith as you diligently practice the victory tools in this book.
- An extra measure of grace, mercy and peace during the restorative process.

Women who have taken steps out of the **"passive aggressive dance"** initially relay they felt stupid, powerless and deceived after realizing they have been entrapped in relationally destructive cycles. On the other hand, I have witnessed light return to the eyes of women as they glimpse hope by having a safe, accountable and balanced listening ear. Over and over women heartily said, *"Thank you for hearing my story. Listening to my reality! I realize I am not losing it. There is truly a name for the repetitive cycles and behaviors I have dealt with for such a long time."* One of the tools towards breaking the silence of passive aggression is to recognize the sabotaging tactics of covert invalidators.

~ SABOTAGING TACTICS of COVERT INVALIDATORS ~

Passive-aggressive people are covert invalidators who use certain behaviors to hide resentments, insecurities and fears. Passive-aggressive patterns linger on because you get caught up in sabotaging cycles. The more you recognize the sabotaging tactics, the quicker you can become proactive. The following are some ways in which this occurs with precision and accuracy.

- **Chaos Junkies**: They create emotional turmoil, physical messes, and confusion. A maddening mix of evasiveness and remorse. Covert invalidators promise to complete tasks or projects, yet, leave them undone or incomplete, which is part of the pattern. Tangible and emotional chaos is created without regard to other's feelings. Women have told me, what drives them up a wall, is this pattern appears to be done intentionally. The delay is to let you know, they will do whatever they want, in their own *"sweet time."* The internal message is *"Nobody is going to tell me what to do."* Ladies, for some passive-aggressives, a certain level of emotional or physical chaos was part of their childhood. Sisters, do not fall into the *trap of chaos*. Instead of engaging in arguments which occur, out of the blue, learn to set healthy boundaries. For example, you may say, *"I would be happy to talk with you. However, if you continue to speak to me that way, I will remove myself from this conversation."*

- **Spinner**: They are masters of twisting other peoples' words to prevent personal exposure or taking ownership of their own actions. Especially, if you attempt to confront issues and bring resolution. Skilled at communicating partial truth or out-right lies. Although, passive-aggressives do not consider them to be lies. These half truths are seen through their grid and it seems right to them. At times, stories will be made up in order to withhold affection, affirmation, information, or love. Female passive-aggressors may spin the truth to get attention, even if it results in emotional chaos. The spin makes them look like a victim, which can hook you. This hook may lead to you initiating *fixing patterns* to prevent relational chaos.

- **Procrastination**: Passive-aggressive people usually procrastinate when a request is made which they do not want to do. Yet, to admit the truth outright is a stretch for them. So they will disregard timetables, unless the request comes from people they have sought after for approval. The message is, *"I am not going to do what you want me to do. I will do it in my own time, or maybe never."* They hope you will get frustrated and do the task yourself. Then, they do not have to feel responsible or do something they did not want to do in the first place.

- **Sarcastic tactics**: If the passive-aggressive senses something is important to you, they will find a way to trivialize your hopes and dreams. Often, out of nowhere, there will be a slight sarcasm expressed. If you confront the sarcastic remarks, the response will be *"What is your problem? I was just kidding."* The subtle, veiled and disguised patterns trigger an internal bubble of emotions. You feel something being stirred up in you .You feel like you are *"loosing your ever-loving mind."* You see crazy making behavior, but can't quite put your *"finger on it."*

- **Mixing it Up**: Passive aggressors are skilled at giving mixed messages, so the receiver of their statements is not quite sure what was stated or intended. Frequently, they will give you the view that your concerns are definitely heard and understood, but then they *"blow off your concerns."*

- **The Hidden and Unspoken Request**: Many times the covert invalidator will appear to be serving you in sincerity; yet, they expect you to do something for them. That expectation is rarely spoken, yet it will surface in an argument, with words such as, *"What have you done for me recently?"* You are standing there with you mouth open, in disbelief. You were not aware of the hidden agenda.

- **Sophisticated Detour Communicator**: The passive-aggressive person is highly skilled in detouring you in conversations, if you are getting too close. They are experts in knowing how to duck an issue or throw a curved ball. Ladies, one of the tools you must learn, is to navigate the detours and stay on subject by saying things like," *I hear what you are saying, but when we are finished discussing _____ , I would be happy to talk about that issue. In the meantime, let's get back to our original discussion."*

- **Boundary Busters**: If you are not clear or strong enough to hold the line of your personal boundaries, the passive-aggressive person will not honor them. In fact, they may question that you have boundaries at all. The saying, give them an inch, and they will take a giant mile over the line, is very true. Once that occurs you have set a precedent, which will be repeated in the future. Remember, though a P-A appears to move on emotionally and relationally, they really don't. They have the memory of an elephant. Though they appear to forget, it is a selective omission and completely protective in origin.

- **Strike Force**: Out of nowhere you experience a rage volcano, which is inappropriate to the issue on the table. You are left stunned. There may be a feeling of being dismissed, shut down or ignored. However, this is done in such a subtle way that you don't know how to process and respond when the passive-aggressive uses a strike force tactic. Then, they will quickly retreat and start communicating to you as though nothing has happened. Once again you are standing there thinking, *"What in the world! This is crazy!"*

*Power Tool:** *"Passive aggression cycles inhibit a person's ability to see the whole story clearly. When any of these tactics creep into your life, stop and take time to evaluate the situation. Ask yourself, which of the above sabotaging behaviors am I dealing with in my relationships? I suggest you write a list of behaviors or patterns you are tolerating.* **It would be a great idea to take some time and journal in order to bring clarity to your thoughts.** *Remember this is a process book and you will need to take pauses along the way.* **Ladies, are you reading the book out loud?**

~ *Prayer* ~

"O, Sovereign Lord! You made the heavens and the earth by your strong hand and powerful arm. Nothing is too hard for you! (Jeremiah 32:17) ~ Ladies, meditate and declare the truth in this word.

Chapter 3

You're not Crazy ~

You're Experiencing Chaotic, Passive-Aggressive Cycles

"Guard your heart above all else, for it determines the course of your life." (Proverbs 4:23)

Although, the relevancy of information in this book is gender-less, my focus is to assist Christian women in breaking the cycles of *generational* passive-aggressive abuses. While this subject matter has been historically silenced in the Christian community, the alarm is sounding and the trumpet is blowing. **It is extremely important for individuals to find, or regain their voices and break the silence**. Emotional, verbal, spiritual and sexual abuses are rarely talked about, or validated, within the Christian community. Sexual and physical abuse has only recently been acknowledged in some denominations of the Christian population. Silence is not golden when it comes to any form of abuse. Emotionally maladaptive parents, raise emotionally wounded and immature children.

It is time for men and women to come out of hiding and bring this topic into the light. People may have heard the phrase passive aggression. However, I have found very few Christians know what it truly is, nor how it manifests relationally. Now, the season has come to identify the unspoken truth underneath passive aggression. For years, Christian women have shared there is a difference between the public and private life of the passive-aggressive men; in their marriage, work, family or male relationships. In counseling women, they timidly remarked, *"Who would ever **believe** the man I am connected to, is not the same gentle, calm guy portrayed in public? Who would believe me if I spoke up about what is really happening behind closed doors? Who would listen to my truth?"*

I have prayed and cried out, that when you come to the last page in this book, you will boldly declare victory. You will also be able to say, **"Deliverance, transformation and healing are mine."** You are a woman of significance, worth and ordained to live out your divine destiny. For such a time as this, you have come into a season of renewal and freedom. It is my desire that you will be refreshed, restored and released to live intentionally while unveiling the silence of oppression, suppression and depression which permeates passive-aggressive relationships.

I am compelled to assist Christian women in the recognition process to break the silence of passive-aggressive relationships with men. However, the responsibility of this book surpasses initial recognition and delves into identifying healthy relationships with men by having a healthy relationship with the Lord. This book may be many things, but it is clearly not a male-bashing book. In fact, my previous book, *Weapons to Stand Boldly and Win the Battle*, is completely dedicated to the equipping and edification of men. No, my sisters, the intent of the book you are reading is to equip you with understanding, so you will be empowered and encouraged.

*Power Tool: *"For the women, who have children, it is my prayer that this book will equip you to break generational passive-aggressive cycles and prevent them from being passed on to sons and daughters. Now is the time! In fact, this may be the right time for you to stop reading and pray for your family."*

~ TIME to REMOVE the MASK ~

Ladies, I realize there has been an assault on the identity and worth of women. Part of the reason for this book, is to empower women with healthy tools to eliminate the patterns of chaos, trauma and abuse. In my culture, whenever a person is experiencing devastating trials, and major drama in their lives, we have a saying which goes like this, *"She is looking toe up from the floor up!"* This means the hurt and drama are starting to show its affects on the person and their pain can be visually recognized. You can see the confusion, despair and bewilderment in their eyes. They are stuck in a spiral of destructive turmoil. Experiencing the impact of chaos is one sign to know a breakthrough is absolutely needed in your life. I pray you do not have to travel that depth of despair, but instead you receive the needed tools to break the damaging cycles.

As women, we face many battles which keep us from experiencing the abundant life the Lord has in store for us. My sisters, we must receive the knowledge to stay unencumbered by harmful generational patterns and behaviors of passive-aggressive people. We must be prepared with practical awareness of spiritual battles, while standing shield-to-shield with each other. In doing so, we will learn the steps towards taking back territory the enemy has stolen. Ephesians 6:10-11 says, *"Be strong in the Lord and in His mighty power. Put on **all** of God's armor so that you will be able to stand firm against **all** strategies of the enemy."* Not some, but all strategies of the enemy will be rendered ineffective, as you walk in truth and put on the full armor of God.

Many women tell me, one of the places they feel sanity restored is at church and in worshipping the Lord in community. At times, they think that if they receive a healing balm of peace; it will calm their minds and it will filter into their hearts. Other times, these same women relate how they can go to church so hurt, so angry and so disillusioned that they sit in a numb state. This can be especially true if the person sitting next to them is the passive-aggressive individual driving them to experience chaos in the first place. For them, the church service comes and goes. It's as if they have to snap out of a daze in order to drive. Leaving church, they head towards an emotionally unsafe place at home. I tell you, the enemy will creep up and rob your joy, even as you sit in church. Dear Ones, it is vital that you educate yourself. It is time to be celebrated and cherished.

My sisters, no matter what you are experiencing right now, there is healing for today and hope for tomorrow. You are worth the fight for freedom. Isaiah reassures us of the love the Lord has for His daughters. **We are on the heart and mind of our Abba Father**. Remember, the power of the scripture in Isaiah 49:16 as you read the remainder of this book. The Lord cares for you so much that He has imprinted your name on the palms of His hands. He will not forsake you, even though, at times, it may feel like He is far away. Know who you are, walk in the truth that you are a royal princess, part of a holy nation, and a daughter of destiny. First Peter 2:9 reminds us as children of the Lord, we are a chosen people. You will find peace and renewed health as you face realities and make new choices which will have lifelong results.

I pray that you will develop a toolkit enabling you to enjoy a life of expectancy, liberty, and anointing. The time is now! It is time to say no more to stress and distress. No more denial! No more silence! No more chaos! No more rationalization! No more abuse! No more mediocrity! No more masks! Are you ready to say, *"I'm stepping into God's best? I am ready to break the silence, remove the mask of protection and any stronghold preventing me from experiencing and developing healthy trusting relationships!"*

*Power Tool: *"I encourage you to stay tuned-in to the voice of the Holy Spirit, as He speaks to you through the material, the scriptures, your prayers and your own life journey. Take the precious nuggets which are meant for you and integrate them in your life. Do not just be a reader or a hearer, but allow yourself to apply the truths which fit your circumstances. When you receive an insight, write it down and evaluate how it may assist you. Then practice, practice,* *and practice again until applying the tools become second nature to you!"*

The journey may feel like you are going through boot-camp, because it will be difficult, but with intentional discipline and the Holy Spirit's guidance, you will be victorious. Breaking rooted patterns requires that you replace old programmed messages in your mind. So, when you learn new ways of thinking and responding, you must *practice*, again and again until you are comfortable. These new tools will eventually become part of your future. This journey has an element of spiritual warfare, because the enemy of our souls does not want you to be free. Yet, the Lord overcame the enemy, and with His help, so can you. You will be triumphant! You are more than a conqueror! *Can I get a halleluiah right about here?*

I have witnessed the pain; prayed for; listened to: and cried with many women through the years. Through their stories, I learned and began to understand how to walk alongside women to restore hope, trust and self-worth. In order to step out of the denial, women must gain awareness and understand their own behaviors in response to the passive-aggressive people in their lives.

Women who live with, or deal with, passive-aggressive people, end up focusing on daily issues and it becomes difficult to see the subtle seduction of the traits and tendencies in their relationships. For example, are you compromising your initially healthy boundaries to avoid making waves? Passive-aggressive wounds are extremely harmful if unchecked. I have learned that women will need to define specific characteristics of passive-aggression they are actually dealing with at home, church, work, or in their families in order to smash the chains of destructive patterns and belief systems.

Contrary to some thoughts in the psychological community, people with passive-aggressive personalities can be restored and develop functionally healthy relationships. However, it takes commitment, honesty, perseverance, and daily vigilance along with hard work. I have seen and worked with women and men who became healed, and maintained consistent accountability, as they walked through a transformation process. As a disciple, or follower of the Lord, it is possible through the power, authority and guidance of the Holy Spirit, to break the chains of passive aggression.

The most effective tools will come through your prayer, faith, and application of the Lord's promises. Then, you will be empowered to stand strong and victorious. The Lord wants you to be actively involved in your own recovery and transformation process. Ladies, you must be very *intentional* in implementing the truth and wisdom the Holy Spirit will impart to you along this journey. His mercy and grace endures forever. Jehovah Rapha means the God who heals. Jehovah Rapha is a restorer and healer of mind, body and soul. Let's be clear, people must choose to be healed and walk through the restorative process. However, you must also know, and declare, that God will not leave, nor forsake you!

People with passive-aggressive personalities often develop a consistent and eventually predictable "unpredictable" set of behaviors, patterns and mood-controlling cycles. This may sound contradictory; however, the reason is because passive-aggressive people attempt to throw you off balance with out of the blue, or unpredictable, behaviors. However, you will begin to see this out-of-the-blue pattern repeat itself in a predictable cycle. Those out-of-the-blue emotional hits will manifest over and over again. Once you get a view of what these patterns look like, and when they occur, you have begun to come out of the *"passive-aggressor's web and world."* Understanding the truth of this covert, or hidden, form of emotional abuse is the first step in unmasking the reality and breaking the silence.

A passive-aggressors behavior cannot be uncovered in a single event. Remember, the best way to identify a relational problem with a passive-aggressive person will be to look for a set pattern of behaviors which are cyclical in nature. For example, let's say you are married and every year around Christmas time you start to feel the tension in the air. It seems like everything is just fine. You go shopping together and then on the way home, out of the blue you are hit. The passive-aggressive person says, *"I don't know why we had to buy all the family, your friends and the children gifts."* You are surprised! Then you share how you thought there had been an agreement on the amount to spend for gifts. You ask why he is so upset, since he was with you all day and said nothing to indicate he was displeased. He then turns to you and says something like, *"You never support me and so it is no use talking with you."* With that, the conversation is over. This is done driving home in the car. The next day is Christmas, and now there is silence and the whole day is filled with stress and tension. You try to make things seem okay for the children's sake. You have just been hit out-of-the-blue. The next holiday rolls around and something similar will occur to sabotage peace in the relationship. *Over time, you can count on experiencing this predictable* **"unpredictable cycle."**

It is important to remember that, once you understand what you are facing, you can activate a proactive plan based on your past observations. You now have retrospective knowledge. Yes, retrospective, because until you can see and break the cycles, you are caught in an entangled web of behavioral patterns. Initially, you do not see, or possibly even believe, the reality. Women struggle to make sense of chaotic environments. You have most definitely been affected by the behaviors, but you have excused and rationalized the reality. Ask the Holy Spirit for discerning wisdom to uncover the repetitive patterns. Remember, we can only change ourselves, not others. Ladies, to walk in clarity and victory means you are required to heal the past wounds sustained in passive-aggressive relationships. Women will have to confront any internal resistance by acknowledging you are experiencing a form of covert abuse and invalidation. Hurt people will definitely hurt people. It will be **essential** to break your own patterns of adjusting, coping and denying that passive-aggressive behaviors exist and have become worse over a period of time.

As women, it might mean viewing the ways you have minimized certain patterns in an attempt to give the passive-aggressive person the benefit-of-the-doubt. This is especially true of Christian women.

A woman with the spiritual gifts of mercy, giving, shepherding or exhorting will have a tendency to try to nurture, rescue and fix others. In doing so, it prevents growth, which comes from experiencing the natural consequences of a person's choices and actions. These spiritual gifts give a person the ability to show compassion, empathy, understanding and long-suffering. The exhortation gift releases the ability for a person to view the potential in others and equip them to reach their purpose.

The person with a spiritual ability of gift-giving is someone who easily gives of their time, resources and possibly finances to assist others in reaching goals and meeting practical needs. However, these spiritual gifts also have what I refer to as a *shadow side*. This side of the gift must be understood. For example, mercy-gifted people have a hard time setting healthy boundaries, because they do not want to hurt anyone. The mercy-gifted person may say yes, when she really needs to say no. If the mercy-gifted person does not monitor her boundaries, she could burnout. As this continues, she also may fill up with resentments. Left unchecked, resentments can spiral to bitterness, which becomes a stronghold paving the way for bondage and un-forgiveness. Another example, the exhorter-gifted person sees people's potential. However, she may *"enable"* them for too long, instead of confronting harmful patterns. This enabling pattern becomes the shadow side of an exhorter.

For years, I have listened to the heartbreak of despair as these beautifully gifted and talented women shared the stories of living with, or being connected to, passive-aggressive men. These same women became isolated and engulfed in this cyclic maze due to the mask they originally wore to cover the truth. This protective facade enabled them to pretend that the pain in their lives did not exist. Constant frustration, unrealistic expectations, broken promises and a different public life seemed to be descriptions of dealing with the passive-aggressive relationships in their lives. Many Christian women have whispered their cries and these same sentiments behind my counseling door. The attempt to bring a rational solution eluded them because the symptoms were so subtle. As they began to work through their own healing path, they could finally detach enough to clearly see the passive-aggressive cycle. The clarity as to why, and how, these relationships remain hurtful and wounding will elude you if you do not choose to step off of the merry-go-round. My sisters, as you emotionally unhook, there will be a lifting of the oppression, veil of secrecy and sadness. Victory will be yours!

In hearing the voices of women, I came to understand how precious it is to have an authentic venue to honestly share and speak truth about their reality. These women had internalized their frustrations and began to lose their God-given identity. This book moves beyond the venue of ink and paper, to release validation to the voiceless, give tools for those in despair, and bring clarity to eliminate feelings of shame or false guilt. I pray women around the world, who suffer under the yoke and unbearable burden of any abusive relationship can learn to live in liberty. I pray women will choose to put an end to the hush-hush reality of passive aggression and speak with candor. Dear Ones, then and only then can women begin the path to becoming unbound from the shackles of passive-aggressive relationships. Remember, healing will take time and work.

The enemy, Satan, has used passive-aggressive behavioral traits since the Garden of Eden. One of the enemy's tactics is to capitalize on generational patterns and unhealthy choices to bring disunity, fear, identity-theft and hopelessness in order to destroy families, marriages and children in the Christian community. This is not a new tactic of the enemy of our souls. However, there is a new blueprint to illuminate this pattern. In the past, passive-aggressive behaviors leading to frustration have been illusive and women were left with a discouraging sense of being in a fog. However, I realized when I started defining and using the term passive-aggressive, women were relieved. Why? It presented some clarity to their reality. Also, the terminology gave them a frame of reference and a distinct place to begin the walk on a path towards freedom. It also allowed the women to finally know they were not *crazy*, but they were living in a chaotic environment. *You cannot heal what you cannot identify or understand.*

Passive-aggressive environments can be painful because they promote self-doubt, destroy relationships, create fear, pile on shame, and ultimately limit a person's God-given abilities. When sabotaging cycles persist, women become physically, emotionally and spiritually sick. Shame, resentment and even bitterness have held them captive. God does not want women to live in a wilderness of bitter bondage. When it comes to abusive cycles the enemy is no respecter of person. He has, and will continue to seek, those whom he can devour, steal from and destroy. Many women are spending years trying to hide, excuse, rationalize and make their lives appear "normal." Yet, these same women strive to conceal the reality under various protective masks.

"Give thanks to the Lord, for He is good! His faithful loves endures forever." (Psalm 118:1)

The main mask, which first emerges, gives the impression **"there is nothing wrong in my life"**, even though there is consistent relational chaos. Typically, these women believe no one sees their pain, and worse yet, no one will validate their plight. Part of the healing journey is to admit the truth and remove the mask to begin healing your brokenness. A dear woman wrote a poem to demonstrate the concept of taking off a protective mask and getting to the real you. As you read this poem out loud pay attention to its truths in your own situation.

Mask Off ~This is the Real Me

My mask keeps slipping out of place.
Yet, I keep catching it – putting it back on my face.
After all, my mask is suppose to hide the real me.
The imperfect, vulnerable one — I don't want people to see.

Oh my, there it goes again, trying to reveal my fragilities.
But with a push of my hand, back in place — the other me.
Don't remember the glimpse of what you just saw.
After all sometimes that person can be real raw.

See me with my mask in place only.
Because with my mask off, I'll seem to be a phony,
Not the person you've come to know.
But another person, who puts on a show.

Oh God, my mask just fell to the ground — split right here.
Now I will have to face my biggest fear.
Mask off — this is the real me.
Will anybody like what they are now able to see?
Printed with permission. ©Sister is a Poet by Rosetta 2004

One day, as explained in this poem, the masks will not stay in place anymore and the life of hurt is exposed. There will be choices to make, such as seeking help to heal as the masks come down. Ladies, it is God's desire that you receive tools to live unencumbered by the drama of abuse. It is time to remove your mask and speak out in order to step into restoration and health.

Chapter 4

Breaking the Silent Cry ~
No Longer Voiceless

"The Lord hears His people when they call to Him for help. He rescues them from their troubles. The Lord is close to the brokenhearted; He rescues those whose spirits are crushed." (Psalm 34:17-18)

Passive aggression is a battle which must be understood from both a natural and spiritual perspective. Anyone who has dealt with passive-aggressive behaviors realizes the term is no longer confined to men in the military, but now permeates other relational connections. Whenever people are seen as being in authority or appear controlling by the passive-aggressive person, then specific defense mechanisms will be displayed. The authority figure may be undermined, blamed or become the target of their negative thinking. Over time, this type of thinking will become a part of their belief system. Once a belief system is in place, it becomes that person's truth, through which they will view certain relationships. Passive-aggressive people are hard to unmask until you learn to identify specific cyclic patterns of behaviors, tactics and characteristics.

Prayerfully, you will learn how to unveil the destructive patterns of passive aggression now, rather than live through more years of frustration, hurt and undefined pain. Forever, I will remember the compelling story of a woman I mentored. She related the following struggle of what it feels like being connected to a passive-aggressive invalidator, who happened to also be a leader in the church.

The Lord sees her, even if she cannot see or feel Him. The Lord sees her, even when she cannot see her own way, because she has lost her sense of direction and identity. The Lord sees her even though she may not see a way out of darkness. She may be walking among other believers thinking that surely someone would be able to help her out of this bleak place of powerlessness. She may want to break the silence, but doesn't feel she can trust anyone. Someone should surely be able to give her the answer to resolve her pain; to resolve her issues. She wants to break the silence, but who can she really trust? When she shares in the Bible Study, everyone prays and after the prayer is done someone says, "I feel like we should do something. We should intervene." However, no one lends a hand or follows through to assist her through the struggle. She even hears someone off to the side say, "I wonder what she did to be in this mess? Girl, you know she needs to be more submissive and supportive."

When I share, no one thinks the issues are all that bad. She asks herself, why they can not see. Why does she feel so alone in a room filled with believing people? Dare I break the silence? Will anyone truly understand? Then a lady, whom she does not know, calls her. In a fog she hears, but also does not really hear. She walks away, because she is so lost. Then the Lord gets her attention so clearly one morning.

The Lord takes her to the book of Matthew, where He reminds her how He takes care of the sparrows. A few days later, she is standing at a bus stop, when she hears a noise. As she looks up, there is a bird in the tree eating. Tears began to flow and she knows that the Lord sees her. He saw her pain, hurt, isolation, despair, and shame. Inside, she can hardly contain herself, as she realizes that El Roi sees her and is changing her heart and healing the layers of pain. That bird was a promise that the Lord would not forsake her. He would take her through a process of renewing her spirit. He would continually draw her close to Him in the process. She eventually finds a place of rest and refuge with her heavenly Father.

At the end of the story she says, "Dee, I know now that I am walking in the grace of a merciful God. I am in the process of unraveling the veil of passive aggression and I am finally seeing the lies I believed for such a long time. The truth has gotten in my heart and I am waking up to the truth. Being connected to passive-aggressive people, over a long period of time, leaves you feeling like you have been sleep-walking; functioning on auto-pilot. Then God wakes you up and the light bulb is flashing."

Although this may not be exactly your story, the sentiments of many women in passive-aggressive relationships can relate.

Matthew 25:44-45 says, *"Lord, when did we ever see you hungry or thirsty or a stranger or naked or sick or in prison, and not help you? Then He will answer, I tell you the truth, when you refused to help the least of these my brothers and sisters, you were refusing to help me."* It is the Lord's desire that faith-based community's minister, and come alongside those who are being abused.

THE NEED IS GREAT ~ A WAKE-UP CALL

Certain days will never be forgotten. One such time created a lasting impression during a conference presentation on spiritual warfare and spiritual gifts. A seminar participant let me know she and her husband had, what she felt were, conflicting spiritual gifts that created additional conflict in their relationship. I moved from the originally planned material and began explaining the reasons for her conflict and the process involved in what she was experiencing. As I spoke, she sensed a surge of emotion from a previous event; often referred to as an **emotional trigger**. As she asked clarifying questions regarding her trigger, she pointed to various sabotaging patterns that impacted her household. This personal interaction of questions and answers drew the crowd to silence as I shared the underlying behavioral roots of the conflict. The room was noticeably silent, blended only with mixed sobs throughout the room. Many conference attendees had also become emotionally triggered and related with the story of conflict.

I waited for the Holy Spirit to direct me and then I made a statement to the group, "Obviously, many of you can relate to what I have just shared!" Their heads shook with agreement. The women's response was clear in their audible sigh of relief. "Finally, a name for the years of stressful, conflict experiences they had endured." Later, others talked about how they could never understand what was happening. They thought no one would ever believe them. They expressed their relief at being understood and finding personal understanding. Similar comments filled the conference hall as loudly a woman proclaimed, "So, I'm not losing my mind!" After hearing similar comments, I spent some time unveiling the truth concerning this insidious epidemic. This subversive epidemic of passive aggression is spreading its tentacles and threatening the fiber of families. It is a topic which has gone underground far too long. During my nursing career, I saw many women and children enter the emergency rooms due to some form of abuse.

A plethora of written information is available concerning domestic violence. Support groups, organizations, legal assistance, safe lodging and counseling centers have sprung up in masses to assist women dealing with violence. However, very little material has addressed passive aggression, especially from a faith-based perspective. Whether we are discussing spiritual, emotional, verbal, physical or sexual abuse, the truth is the incidences of passive aggression are rising significantly within society. The Christian community is not immune to the ills of society or the impact of this devastating, and often immobilizing, entity revealed through passive aggression. Ladies, we must speak from the heart and get as real as we can, so the faith-based community will understand and become proactive.

Passive-aggressive people have not observed any modeling of positive communication; where they see negative emotions expressed in healthy ways. The people may not be aware of how deeply repressed their feelings are buried and covered by anger and resentment. A passive-aggressive person will be surprised, discouraged and shocked when you attempt to address a behavior. The men I have worked with tell me they have felt misunderstood. They feel afraid people will see straight through their vulnerabilities. Most of the time, if a person is physically hit or experiences rage toward them, no one has to be told there is abuse involved. People know it! There is a sense deep down in your gut! It is plain as day. Now, when it comes to passive aggression, which falls under covert emotional abuse, it is more difficult to identify. The subtle factors involved in passive aggression leave people guessing when is the next bomb going to be dropped.

While often misunderstood, patterns of passive aggression will become clearer as you define and recognize its characteristics and roots. By nature, the passive-aggressive personality erupts in concealed ways, which weakens and potentially destroys relationships. It is the heart of the Lord for His sons and daughters to not **deafen the cries** of those being abused in any form. Nor would He want apathy to persist, which only serves to perpetuate abuse. If abuse in any form is permitted, it destroys families and consequently has long term affects on men, women, children and society as a whole.

Passive aggression has grown and frequently gone undetected in Christendom due to the silence, shame, fear and the confusion of women who are impacted by this subversive behavior. In the faith-based community, passive-aggressive behavior can manifest itself anywhere from the bishop in the robe, to the pastor in the pulpit, to the man in the pew. Passive aggression is only one of the ways the enemy has capitalized on as an inroad into Christian relationships. Pornography, addictions of all sorts, divorce and other societal problems are currently on the upsweep in faith-based communities.

Christian women, who are connected with passive-aggressive men, need a safe way to express the truth of their situation and learn effective tools to redirect and defuse personal invalidation. Sadly, the church has not always been an emotionally safe place. I have worked with hundreds and hundreds of woman through the years in the Christian community and they have felt guilty, frustrated and ashamed. Ladies, as you proceed through this material, know that **awareness** will be important, but **application** of the tools will set you free. Frequently, passive-aggressive patterns remain hidden, silenced, minimized or avoided within Christendom and are first made visible in the home or workplace. Women in the faith-based community are silent partly due to the subtleness of passive aggression. As the Christian community seeks awareness and knowledge of this pervasive problem, the issues surrounding this epidemic can be revealed; put into the light. Once in the light the journey to healing can unfold. *As believers, we are called to be conquerors, not compromisers.* You will have to practice and practice the tools over time to see tangible change and experience liberty.

I am hopeful, as faith-based communities familiarize themselves with understanding of abusive relationships, they will provide safe refuge environments for women to break their silence of various forms of abuse. **If the faith-based community takes steps toward gaining training, awareness and strategies to create proactive action, it will permit**:

- The ability to recognize the traits and characteristics of passive-aggressive cycles.
- The ability to implement practical ways to validate women's reality and pain.
- The development of supportive and safe transforming places for disclosing various forms of abuse.
- The development of ministries, which provide recovery tools to circumvent passive-aggressive patterns from being passed on to sons, daughters and grandchildren.
- Training seminars to provide educational classes that bring an understanding of the path and origin of passive-aggressive behavior.
- Equipping principles of spiritual warfare tactics and strategies in breaking generational passive aggression.

- A safe place in the church, giving voice to women all over the world.

~ REALITY CHECK ~

The passive-aggressive personality was rooted as a result of emotional, physical, verbal, painful, or traumatic family systems. A child learns to repress their true feelings out of fear of being shamed or overly punished. Adults, who were brought up in emotionally and relationally chaotic homes, experienced an unhealthy communication model. These adults, who were wounded in childhood, are now stuck back in time. In other words, children who grew up in these environments stop their emotional growth at the age of recognizing or feeling their hurt and perceived, or real, injustice. Usually this takes place when the person becomes a teenager. If the adult does not mature, they will remain emotionally childish in some areas of their life. Women often relate that they are dealing with a "little boy." Deep inside this adult is an "unhealed little boy" who is emotionally unavailable and cannot permit anybody to get emotionally close. Displaying passive-aggressive traits is a way to deflect the intensity of feelings and recover a false security to camouflage their inability to be emotionally intimate with others.

Let's look at an example of how emotional wounds develop and play out over time:

A thirteen year old child, who has an alcoholic father exhibiting rage and anger every time the weekend approaches, will likely become an adult who shows unhealthy behavior when the weekend is approaching. For example, each weekend the boy's alcoholic father binge drinks and become verbally abusive. The father then calls the boy names and makes shameful statements to him such as; "You're a wimp who will never amount to anything. You are just another drain on my pocketbook." At the time, the child is not allowed to respond to the hurtful statements; giving no voice. Nor did he have permission, or freedom to say he is angry about the hurtful put downs, even when he has now become a teenager. At this point, the boy stops his emotional growth at the age of thirteen. Now, as an adult, any perceived criticism is felt through the filter of the thirteen year olds past hurt, buried anger, resentment and pain. The adult may then become passive, passive-aggressive or aggressive. Many become a combination of all three. Over time, if the root causes of buried anger are not dealt with, an **event-reactive pattern** *becomes embedded and will be seen time and time again, in relationships at home, ministry, work or family system.*

Hiding emotions of hurt and anger may have been a survival skill as a child. Childhood survivor thinking has the distinct potential of becoming relationally problematic as an adult. In my coaching practice, I have seen many situations where the person is unaware that he/she is operating passive aggressively. The passive-aggressive person frequently has a child-like, or immature, hunger to experience love and affirmation from others. Yet, they are afraid of being too dependent on others relationally. Therefore, they sabotage intimate relationships by avoiding responsibilities, obligations or promises to others. This leads to being emotionally unavailable to others. There is a fear of intimacy with significant others. Yet, deep down, they long to know how to be intimate with others.

Significant others are connected, but rarely does the passive-aggressive person let people get too close, so they institute passive-aggressive traits as a way of averting exposure. They have not learned to manage, or accept anger, which is where blame comes into play. It is hard to believe that a person will get their needs met at your expense, regardless of whether or not it is consciously done. Periodically, passive aggression towards others is done intentionally. In other situations, it is so integrated into their personality that even the passive-aggressive person is unaware of the impact of their actions.

It is very hard to identify a passive-aggressive person because the truth is they have learned to be sneaky or deceptive. Passive-aggressive people act one way in public, but function in a totally different way in private. There are paradoxes in viewing their behavioral patterns. Although, they avoid confrontation like the plague, they equally cannot resist giving you a message which fosters conflict. The messages communicate, *"I am displeased with you or with something you have done to me."* **In actuality, these unspoken passive-aggressive messages may appear like any of the following:**

- Shaking their head, giving a nonverbal message which says, *"I am frustrated with you."*
- Rolling their eyes which send the message, *"Here we go again!"*
- Heavy sighs or long pauses, after you ask them a question which gives the message, *"What now?"*
- Statements to throw you off balance: *"Is complaining all you can do? Why can't you just get over it? Why are you making such a big deal out of nothing?"* The message is an attempt to get you to question or doubt yourself.

******Power Tool****: "If you have encountered any of these unspoken messages, take time and journal your thoughts about the circumstances. As you describe the circumstances, do not forget to record how you felt and what action you took at the time. This is a good time to ask the Holy Spirit to help you respond in healthy ways in the future."*

Women have told me, when they experience these subtle messages they frequently feel foolish for feeling hurt. Some women shared they began doubting their reality and blowing it off, by saying; the behavior is just too trivial; *"Why even bring it up?"* If these communication patterns persist over long periods of time; the women know something is wrong, but can't put their finger on it. However, they now feel rejected, used or betrayed. Since, passive-aggressive people rarely say, *"I'm sorry"*, it is hard to bring resolution to situations in the relationship. The main reason there is no apology is because they believe there has been an injustice done to them. The passive-aggressive person loves to hear you ask them, *"What's wrong?"* Then they know the subtle messages were effective and you are captured into the **bait, hook and reel in** tactic of manipulation. Ladies, you are being taught a lesson, with this ever-so-subtle nonverbal style. Once you take hold of the behavioral patterns, you will be able to break the cycle for yourself.

The passive-aggressive person attempts to avoid arguments or disagreements. In addition, they try to steer clear of expressing true inner thoughts or dealing directly with perceived or real confrontation. Utilizing passive-aggressive defense mechanisms is a device to control situations and people without outwardly appearing to be controlling. The skill a passive-aggressive person has been so developed, they can stay behind the veil of being a *"nice guy"* to the outside world. Emotionally protective survival skills, learned early in life, become completely integrated into the individual's personality. Thus, this is one of the reasons for the blindness of people who have become passive aggressive. I will discuss additional information concerning roots of passive-aggressive characteristics, traits and tendencies, later in the book.

The passive-aggressive person has learned this form of coping to prevent others from seeing feelings of insecurity and fear. **One of the tools in dealing with passive-aggressive people is to recognize the behavior as soon as possible**. I have devoted an entire chapter to the actual traits and tendencies of passive-aggressive people, along with tools to address specific behavioral patterns. The following list gives you a starting place in activating the "**recognition tool**." People act in passive aggressive ways when they:

- Conceal hostility by appearing to be nice to others they dislike, fear or feel insecure around, yet are unskilled in verbalizing honestly with that person. Often mutters to themselves.
- Appear to agree to do something, yet do not follow through with promises, because they really did not support the idea in the first place.
- Attempt to have others assume responsibility for decisions, thereby, avoiding accountability for the end results. In doing so, they can appear to be the "good guy."

- Tell others what they want to hear, even if they do not believe what they have stated.
- Take opportunities to "put others down" in a sarcastic or humorous manner and then say they were "just kidding."
- Deny personal interactions which are becoming destructive.
- Communicate statements which are inconsistent with behavioral patterns.
- Consistently make excuses for why they forgot a request.
- Withdraws if feel requests made of them are unfair. Then will use subtle sabotage to get even.
- Sees people who are perceptive, as being a threat, critical, controlling and judgmental.
- They live in fear-of-failure thinking.
- Attempts made to defeat other people's requests by failing. Therefore, others will become frustrated and pick up the slack for them. This rescuing cycle gives a false perception that they do not have to take responsibility. This tendency will occur at home, families, at work and in ministries.

*Power Tool: *"Ladies, did any of these ring a bell? Be sure to journal which ones, and how it affects you?"*

Take a few minutes to review the next list and journal about typical reactions to passive-aggressive experiences in your life. Many times women experience a variety of emotions in response to the above statements. When they do recognize the impact of passive aggressiveness they may:

- Experience frustration because of the inconsistency of the behavior.
- Experience resentment because of the dishonesty.
- Experience a weariness and emotional burnout.
- Experience anger and distrust as promises are constantly broken and rationalized.
- Experience confusion, surprise and disillusionment.
- Experience hypersensitive and reactive feelings, especially if children are involved.

- Experience detachment in order to protect against further hurt and disappointment.
- Learn to confront the behaviors and patterns by setting healthy boundaries.
- Learn to address inconsistencies in words and actions.
- Learn to stop enabling, rescuing, excusing and fixing.
- Learn to respect self and become safe for others.

*Take Note: *"The above are normal and healthy. They will propel you to break the denial and break your own cycle. Healing can take place with honesty and openness, as you seek the help you need to walk the journey towards restoration."*

As children, we have all heard the saying, "sticks and stones can break my bones, but names will never hurt me." We had it all wrong, because most definitely sticks and stones can break our bones through a physically abusive person. Words can wound and break our hearts, through the verbally abusive person. Decide today to stop the cycles.

Christian women learn to adjust, adjust, adjust, and to compromise, compromise, and compromise again, until their own identity is stolen and they wake up one day hurt, angry, bewildered and feeling powerless. Waves of fear and shame overtake them and thoughts such as, "If I tell, will the church support or believe me?" Thus, grief sets-in and the truth is stifled from coming out. So, hurt is buried alive and the passive-aggressive cycles goes on until the silence is broken. As you are reading, you have already begun to break the silence, even if it is simply head knowledge at the moment.

Women, who believe they are not being physically or sexually harmed, will tend to deal with their emotionally abusive situations in silence. Yet, the reality is, emotional abuse cuts and wounds deeply, and at times, can be more devastating than any other form of abuse. Learning to recognize passive-aggressive behaviors and setting boundaries will be critical in enjoying healthy and respectful relationships. When you know what you are dealing with, you can take steps to make a change. We may not be able to alter other people's behaviors, but we most definitely have control over our own responses and actions. Take a closer look at how you may be contributing to a passive-aggressive environment by not utilizing your voice and responding assertively.

As you read on, I pray you will come out of your silence, restore confidence and choose to be healed. Psalm 34:17-18 says, *"The Lord hears His people when they call to Him for help. He rescues them from their troubles. The Lord is close to the brokenhearted; He rescues those whose spirits are crushed.* I love this statement! It is very comforting. After reading this, I re-read it and put my name in the passage and personalized the truth. Try it and see what happens to you.

The person dealing with a passive-aggressive person has their perception of reality minimized, denied or rejected. This frequently leaves the woman with self doubt concerning her reality. Until you understand this behavior, it is hard to identify specifics, and learn to respond in healthy ways to bring about change and healing. Without the truth of the underlying roots and tools to proactively respond to passive aggression, women are left believing, "What can I do?"

The passive-aggressive individual is capable of distorting rational thinking. You think you are using rational solutions; however, you are dealing with irrational and distorted filters. Frequently, you do not know what has happened to you, other than you feel internally lousy and can't answer why. Do you know someone like this?

My sisters, I want to repeat, that if you have been dealing with a passive-aggressive person in your life, realize: **You Are Not Crazy**! The chaos and confusion of these relationships is real! The personal healing and triumph will emerge as you come face to face with the reality of your relationship. It is time to commit to being consistent, in taking steps towards personal restoration and develop a *proactive* toolkit. There is a bona fide pattern of behaviors occurring in your life. **Now is the time of the Lord's favor**. In order to move forward in the healing process, women will eventually have to ask: *"What made you come alive on the outside? This means you will need to dig up the root of what you have lost on the inside. What is blocking you?"* It is time to stop here and doing a bit of journal writing.

Passive aggression has gone concealed and has only recently begun to be addressed. As more and more safe transforming places become available, it will enable women to step up, step out and break their masked silence. In doing so, women's pain will be validated. Truth concerning the personality of passive aggression will help to avert sabotaging our future relationships.

*Power Tool: *"As you get real, in order to heal, surround yourself with safe people who build you up and do not use words to tear you down. Safe people support and value you enough to speak truth with love. Safe people have your best interest at heart. Safe people do not shame and condemn you. Safe people do not punish you for the purpose of meeting their needs."*

If you are suffering with inner turmoil because you live, work and struggle to survive within passive-aggressive relationships, it will be important to ask and answer the following questions. ***This is not an inclusive list, yet it is a place to start.***

- *Why is he so angry? What did I do to make him treat me the way he does?*
- *He professes to love me, so why does he talk to me with such an irritated or harsh tone?*
- *Why is it, that if I ask him to do something for me, he sounds supportive, and then uses sabotaging patterns such as procrastination? He may even say yes, but does not follow through.*
- *Why is it that if I try to get concerns addressed, they remain unresolved?*
- *Why do I feel guilty when I don't even know what I did?*
- *Why is my boss undermining my efforts to be an effective team member?"*

As you continue to read the material, answers to the above questions will be uncovered. You will see relational aspects that have burdened you in coping with a passive-aggressive husband, boss, boyfriend, or father. A big part of receiving freedom is to be able to spot the behavior. When passive aggression remains unchallenged and concealed, it gives permission to remain subversively destructive.

My sisters, a life which is set free is an awesome sight to behold. Women must be healed of the hurts and harmful wounds of living a life of oppression, doubt and fear. Declare that you are designed to reach your fullest potential and destiny. The Lord promises to strengthen you for the journey. Philippians 4:13 says, *"For I can do everything through Christ, who gives me strength."*

*Power Tool: *"Speak these words out loud whenever you need to be encouraged and empowered."*

The passive-aggressive man has not healed from his past and you are reaping the harvest of unchecked wounds. Pray that God will sustain you as you walk through, and out, of the gates of the *"world of a passive-aggressive"* person. As you continue to read, we'll address methods of personal validation, so you are able to sustain and persevere. Press on my sisters! All of heaven is ready to assist you in living triumphantly.

~Prayer ~

"Lord, thank you for helping me to discern the truth concerning my relationships. I realize it is the truth which will set me free. I choose to praise you regardless of circumstances. Jehovah Shalom, I pray for an outpouring of your grace and peace in my life. Let your peace rule in my heart today. Thank you for helping me. I know, as your daughter, you will equip me to begin the cycle of breaking the silence.

Chapter 5

Hallmark Patterns ~

Lifting the Veil

"Give your burdens to the Lord, and He will take care of you . . ."
(Psalm 55:22)

Why are sisters all over the world dealing with the frustration and pain of men who sabotage intimacy? Let's take some time to untangle the truth from the sabotage. Consequently, you will learn to identify the toxicity of passive aggression. Our focus now is to expose and bring clarity to four classic patterns; the silent treatment, the accusation game, the great dismissal and flipping the script. Time and time again I have heard women relate stories about their husbands, bosses, pastors, brothers, fathers or sons. There are similar threads of crazy-making and sabotaging patterns in their relational stories. These cyclical patterns are described consistently whenever women attempt to identify passive-aggressive traits, tactics and tendencies.

~ THE SILENT TREATMENT ~

"How long will you torment me? How long will you try to crush me with your words?" (Job 19:2)

One of the crazy-making tactics known as the **silent treatment** is definitely a classic trademark of the passive-aggressive person.

They tend to cut you off from talking if they feel too vulnerable. They take on a silent stance. This learned behavioral pattern is driven by repressed childish anger, which was suppressed by childish fears. The myth is the person is being quiet. However, the truth is, passive-aggressive people learned to use defense mechanisms to prevent further wounding. Remember, passive aggressors are aggressive in a passive way, which is why you get mixed messages while communicating. This behavior was integrated as a coping, or protective mechanism, very early in childhood. As a child, the passive-aggressive person was shamed, humiliated or minimized in some fashion. After being hurt, attempts were made to express their feelings which were not heard or validated by a parent or significant person. Over a period of time, if invalidation is persistent, the person learns to shut down emotionally. The common thought was it is not okay to share emotions. These beliefs turned into denying resentment, hurt, fears, insecurities and anger.

When a passive-aggressive invalidator feels rejected, attacked or emotionally threatened in any way, this shutting down pattern of silence is set in motion. It is a distorted way of getting a message across to the person they perceive as having hurt them. *"You hurt me and I am not going to give you the time of day by talking to you."* It becomes a matter of injustice for them. As a child, they felt a need to protect themselves from hurt and rejection. Additionally, becoming silent was the child's attempt to disown their part in any tension or discomfort in their significant relationships. This silent behavior gave the child a false sense of control. Now as an adult, this cycle is duplicated every time there is a sense of injustice.

Sometimes, passive-aggressive people are paying someone back for a real, or perceived, threat to their personhood. Passive aggressors believe they do not owe you an explanation or an apology for any way they hurt you. It will translate emotionally to you like, "You are not worth my time or attention." At an earlier age, when the passive-aggressive child was hurt physically or emotionally, they did not receive comfort. Most of the time, if someone verbally hurt the child, there was no ownership or apology given for their actions. This pattern will be carried into adulthood. Thus, anytime the passive-aggressive person feels rejected, attacked or threatened during potential conflict, they will try to find a way to protect in a world of silence.

The silent treatment is a form of pouting and playing the victim, or "**little boy**." It may be in response to an imagined slight or to a really shameful event. Nonetheless, it causes internal turmoil. For example, the passive-aggressive person is upset about something, but is fearful of expressing their true feelings. Many P-A people are afraid of losing control in their relationships. The more significance or authority the person has to them, the more fear is ingrained. Covert or hidden emotional abuse can manifest without a word such as with the use of the silent treatment. Several of my clients have coined this controlled behavior the **"wounding silent treatment."**

In the majority of cases, this pattern develops because it's what the emotional abuser experienced growing up. For example, his mom or sister may have given him a task. He was told, *"Don't forget to stop and get the washing detergent on your way home from school."* When he arrives home after football practice without the detergent he is told, *"You forgot the detergent again?"* The P-A interprets that statement as, *"You are so irresponsible. You are so stupid! Why couldn't you remember that one thing? Can't you do anything right?"* After a while, the person believes the lie that he cannot measure up to other people's expectations. Anytime you question a passive-aggressive man, they hear you through the grid of a filter. The filter in his head is saying, *"Why is she questioning me? She has no right to question me! She is such a know-it-all!"*

The passive-aggressive person never learned or developed constructive life skills for handling negative emotions, conflict resolution, or exercising productive decision making skills. It is difficult for them to resolve events which may expose their weaknesses, insecurities, shame and fears. They rarely acknowledge when they are wrong or ask forgiveness after hurting others. The silent treatment is used whenever the person feels some level of internal discomfort or powerlessness. A retaliation tactic is to express crushing and confusing words, hoping to derail a person's direction and ultimately avoid confrontation or exposure.

The silence can last for several days, weeks, or even months. If you are the victim of this treatment, it creates a very helpless feeling as you live with the ache of a **silent void**. If you are experiencing the silent treatment, tell the person you are aware of the attempt to get even with you for some perceived or real injustice. Then, my sisters, get on with your day until they come out of their pouting. The person will need to develop more mature ways of handling emotions. Be assertive and share with the covert aggressor what you expect. They do not like being held accountable for their behavior. Be ready for the counter attack. It is good to hear what they have to say, so you know what tools to implement.

One unforgettable woman shared an insightful and heart-breaking story about the silent treatment. She hadn't realized the length or impact of the isolation within the family home, until her child said, ***"Dad shuts himself in, thinking he is shutting us out."*** That utterance of truth followed nine weeks of no legitimate conversations from the passive-aggressive father. This type of repetitive, extreme behavior makes women scream inside saying, *"I can't play this game!"* When this happens, no one speaks. Year after year of trying to deal with the silent treatment can harden hearts. Over time, frustrated and irritated tones of voice become noticeable to others. Women tell themselves, if he doesn't speak, I don't have to either. This is not the comfortable silence shared when two people lovingly work alongside one another. No, if the passive-aggressive person senses an exposure of some sort or if they will be upstaged in anyway, the silent treatment becomes an *unfair fighting mechanism.* It is their attempt to punish the other person for their actions or for not perceiving, or meeting their needs.

The passive-aggressor suddenly emerges from their cave of silence and says something like, *"I'm leaving now, see you later,"* or they will leave a note on the refrigerator telling you where they are going. In their minds they have now reconnected with you. In their mind this is making an effort for reconciliation. If women do not respond to that attempt, the silent treatment may continue. Thus, absolutely nothing is resolved. The woman is walking around hurt and the passive-aggressive person gets up one day, saying things like "*What is wrong with you?*"

The passive-aggressor quickly moves on. Ladies, this is why you must use the tool of addressing issues as close to the event as possible. Remember P-A people often believe their lives are controlled by others; however, they lack the skills to be assertive. To minimize their attacks, you must learn to be assertive. Most passive-aggressors will have a difficult time dealing with others who will openly and truthfully call them out on their behavior. We are responsible for our own actions. Passive-aggressive people can create chaos and yet they move on while acting as though nothing has happened. So, if you share later, they will frequently feel like you are attacking them. A statement they will make is, "*What are you talking about?*" They may even deny having said anything resembling your memory of a situation. Now, what do you do if the silent treatment has already begun?

My sisters, as the repetitive cycle reaches the point where you believe you must try harder, the journey of pain has already taken a toll. Dealing with passive aggression is a relational and spiritual issue. The enemy, known by most as Satan, is also called the Adversary. He is one who shows no mercy and will infiltrate and capitalize on peoples' pain. Another name for the enemy is Beelzebub, literally meaning, the Lord of the Flies. He is one who will feed on your hurts, disappointments and frustrations, which turns into strongholds or bondages. If unchecked, the enemy is capable of taking you down a slippery slope towards the bondages of resentment and bitterness. If you aren't aware or don't have accountable people in your life, your heart may harden and allow bitterness to settle into the very core of your being. As this happens, silence becomes more normal and the silent treatment seems the easiest route within the relationship to "keep the peace." If you are not alert, you may start responding to situations in passive-aggressive ways.

If resentment and bitterness is not healed because you are trying to prevent further emotional injury, eventually, you'll get up one morning and not even recognize yourself. You may even develop passive aggressive traits yourself. I pray, as you recognize passive-aggressive characteristics and take ownership of your own response patterns, you will not continue the trail down that slippery slope of bondage. One of the tactics covert aggressors do is accuse everyone outside of them as being the cause of their internal, emotional discomfort, or pain. The accusation game is another hallmark characteristic.

~ THE ACCUSATION GAME ~

"They do not talk of peace; they plot against innocent people who are minding their own business." (Psalm 35:20)

As time marches forward, and behavioral patterns become entrenched, an "*accusation game*" becomes apparent. Each person in the passive-aggressive dance of emotions becomes familiar with their role and the *supposed* spoken and unspoken rules. I say *supposed*, because in the passive-aggressive person's mind, they believe that they have spoken many thoughts to you, however, it is not true. This is part of the reason, at times, you feel like you are losing your righteous mind. **When honesty is not prevalent in relationships, it is very easy to experience frustration and be hurt by accusatory remarks**. Unfortunately, no one wins when blame and dishonesty prevail. The outcomes of the "*accusation game*" are emotional abuse with a sprinkling of innuendos and harsh argumentative tones.

There are various passive-aggressive tactics used to prevent conflict and cause your eventual silence. When silence occurs on your part, it means you have become neutralized. The purpose of you becoming silent is you are sick and tired of being sick and tired. Neutralizing a person is a common passive-aggressive way of shutting you down verbally and emotionally. At times, you attempt to rationalize the person's accusatory statements. Falsely, Christian women say, "*He really doesn't see what he has done to me. He doesn't mean it; he had such a traumatic or hard upbringing. I must show more compassion. Jesus would be empathetic, wouldn't he? At work, you may hear I don't understand what her problem is about; all I have done is help.*" Women then go along enabling the drama and trauma in this destructive relationship for years on end. In other words, the accusation game is played with no winner and the drama continues.

After a particularly chaotic season, you may ask the passive-aggressive person to go to counseling, or the human resource department at work, and all you receive is denial. He may tell you, "*We don't need counseling; we just need to do the right thing, the Christian thing.*" Obviously, the statement in and of itself appears to be reasonable. So, you force yourself to interject a flicker of hope, only to have the little light of hope blown out for lack of follow through. If you bring the subject up in the future, the person has convinced themselves that they are doing "just fine," and believe you do not want to acknowledge how hard they have tried. The man has convinced himself that because he shared, that action alone was the solution. Likely though, there were no tangible steps taken towards resolution.

At the workplace, you may hear a co-worker say, "*This is your problem and you need to fix it.*" If you go to the human resource department, they advise you to meet with your manager. So you set up an appointment, and when you walk into their office, the passive-aggressive person is already there. Taken aback, the atmosphere does not appear to be safe and so you guard your words. After the meeting you request a separate meeting and the manager, states, "*It seems as though, you can not let this issue go. I suggest you work it out with the other person.*" You feel stuck, because the other person is passive-aggressive. All of the examples you communicated are subtle and it made no sense to the manager. In this situation, it is important to document and recognize the *predictable cycles*, so you can become proactive in your responses.

~ Weary of the Accusation Game ~

Women tell me it wears heavily on them to continually receive empty promises. If they remind the passive-aggressive person, often they are met with denial the promise was ever made. Other times, there is a re-promising with a procrastination time lapse. For example, if the man agreed to stop yelling and then he loses it over you asking a simple question, the promise holds no merit. The man may say something like, "*See, even when I am trying, it is not good enough, and so I guess my efforts are not worth it to you. I keep trying to put myself out there and it is not appreciated by you.*" They may even have the audacity to suggest you should go to counseling alone because you need to "*deal with your own issues.*"

Seasons of uncertainly create "*the crazies.*" The passive-aggressive person, who is all of a sudden, understanding, lovable, or very nice to you makes you think things have changed. Things flow on an even keel for a long period of time. Then, with one quick, laser precision hit, he creates chaos with criticism, sarcasm, insinuations or angry rage. You try to get to the root of it and he may say, "*What do you mean?*" Uncertainty has now been released in your mind. "*Now, what do I say and do?*" These types of repetitive situations may push the Christian woman to do a great deal of personal introspection, until finally her false conclusion states that he must be right, and she must try harder and encourage him more. *At that very moment, Ladies, the cycle of despair is set in motion.* The silent inward journey begins to seep in your spirit once again. The result of this consistent cycle is a feeling of powerlessness, created by self-doubt. As you read on, you will discover additional tools to address passive-aggressive behaviors and patterns.

Ladies, learning to address this pattern, before it is engrained, will prevent you from spiraling down the destructive path of painful emotions. You must begin by practicing various skills. One is a skill called rephrasing. You calmly reword what is said with a clarifying statement such as, "*Ok, let me see if I understand you. This is what I heard . . .*" Even though, this sounds like psycho babble, it is vital in detaching. It will stop you from using old patterns of communication, which hook you. Also, keep in mind, the passive-aggressive person has an innate desire to be heard and understood. This tool will allow for untangling of words and promote calmness within the chaos. The third hallmark pattern is one I call, *"the great dismissal."*

~ THE GREAT DISMISSAL ~

"Hope deferred makes the heart sick, but a dream fulfilled is a tree of life." (Proverbs 13:12)

Likely, you remember a time when you were right in the middle of a discussion with a passive-aggressive person and they stop and say, *"I am not going to talk to you about this anymore!"* When a passive-aggressor is experiencing a conflict, there is a tendency to dismiss you from their eyesight, if they sense you will question, challenge or expose any fears. At times, this may literally be a dismissal with a hand motion. In other situations, the person will walk out in the middle of a conversation, creating a multitude of unspoken messages in your mind. This hallmark behavior is intended to shut you out, and shut you up anyway they can, to avoid having to discuss an issue. Passive-aggressive men do not want to risk the potential that you may be right, because they believe that would make them wrong. This is based on a black and white or all-or-nothing filter. For others in the faith-based communities, it may be a shame-based filter of legalism.

Dear ones, stop for a minute and put your hand up in front of your face and spread your fingers apart. You will notice, you can see, but you have blind spots. If you try to look through any of the fingers for any length of time, it will appear to be blurry. This is the view of the passive-aggressive person. They have a filtered view of life and people. Now ladies, take your hand down. You notice the view is now clear. Anytime a person communicates to an unhealed passive-aggressive man, they can anticipate a veiled filter system. The passive-aggressor believes they have a clear view and yet, it is a blind spotted view.

The dismissal technique is a learned behavior which was modeled and developed at some point during developmental stages of childhood, which is now being practiced as an adult. Underneath this dismissal behavior pattern is usually some form of toxic shame. People who have experienced toxic shame believe they are inherently flawed and defective as a human being. As a result, shame-based people tend to believe others see them as being unworthy. A feeling of inadequacy and fear develops, and unhealthy belief systems will emerge in relationships. For example; a person may have come from a workaholic family with an abusive parent. Frequently, there was verbal rage in the home. Let's say this child was shamed at age twelve for some innocent act. Now, if the child continues to experience shaming or critical statements well into adulthood, a self-judging belief system will be rooted. Thus, every time that adult feels inferior, insecure or ashamed, they will react emotionally and relationally as a twelve year-old would react, regardless of their chronological age.

It's as if the personal trauma arrests emotions and holds them captive, even though physical development continues into adulthood. I call this arresting development; **season of frozen emotions**. A pattern then forms where circumstances that involve similar emotions take the individual right back to the coping skills learned in earlier events. This is also referred to as **triggering**. So, the emotional age of a person is really defined by the point where they took on messages about themselves in a perceived, or real, traumatic situation. This becomes the age at which they emotionally and relationally function as an adult. The feelings of not measuring up or letting others down is internally controlling their thoughts, beliefs, and behaviors. The protective tool of pushing you away will happen except within the presence of the passive-aggressive person's family of origin. Why? The person wants to be seen as the *"nice guy"* in their family.

Ladies, if you have been impacted by a passive-aggressive person, you have developed protective mechanisms to prevent further pain. You also may begin to bury your true feelings since it is not safe to express or show emotions. You'll need to watch for your own level of frozen emotions. The passive-aggressive man has frozen emotions from his past early childhood development. The woman, however, develops frozen emotions to protect herself from the fall-out of being in a passive-aggressive relationship.

Passive-aggressive personalities desire to be seen within the confines of their family of origin, as the even paced person. The fear of rejection and further abandonment by the family pushes out the "*gentleman persona.*" The passive-aggressive person feels they cannot risk losing the "nice person" perception of their family of origin. They realize the family can never see their angry and hurt behavior. Later in your reading, we'll take a look at the specific roles and family dynamics that play into this subtle pattern. Some people say the P-A is like a Dr. Jekyll and Mr. Hyde personality; presenting a nice persona to those in public and behaving another way in private. Other times, there are rapid and radical mood swings. Although, this behavior is classic in the family, it can be manifested in the workplace and faith-based communities. **For now, suffice to say, the dismissal skill is a detour strategy to prevent anyone in perceived control or authority from seeing their fears and insecurities.**

Additionally, the great dismissal involves false bonding when opportunities arise for real friendship. If this is a male child and the father-bond was done in a critical manner, at certain stages of development, the child stops maturing. If, for example, the father was an alcoholic and the child lived from day to day not knowing how the father would respond to the family, the outcome becomes emotional masking. Seeds of anger and resentment develop in the child, which one day erupts and spews onto others. This child, or teenager, loses his sense of identity and security. Therefore, he will fight to retain his survival instincts and dismisses others so they do not get close enough to see personal vulnerability.

The passive-aggressive child did not form a healthy concept of who they were as individuals. For that reason, they begin to become whatever others need them to be. For example, if a parent within a family conveyed messages that made the child feel they let them down; the child begins to question their ability to measure up to others' standards and expectations, perceived or real. ***As adults, if anyone even asks them clarifying questions, they hear it through the filter of accusation.*** They then will become defensive and use dismissing language on the person they believe is challenging them to make them look bad. Since, it was not safe to express hurt or angry emotions in their childhood home, they feel the need to survive and protect them by dismissing others in adulthood.

There may have been some form of daily chaos in the childhood home. Thus, the child begins to guess at what are normal expectations. Some children become the lost child. This child tries not to make visible waves in the family of origin, by becoming manipulative. That child learns to control in very distinct manipulative ways. This destructive method of manipulating will continue into adulthood. They will say things as an adult to their own children that manipulate behavior. Statements such as, *"Do it for daddy, or why are you doing that, when you know it makes me upset?"* Some fathers emotionally blackmail their children to attend family functions. Even as adult children, the father will have power over them by saying things like, *"Are you coming to the family function? You don't want to be responsible for breaking the tradition, do you?"* Mind you, if you confront the passive-aggressive behavior with what they are saying, it will be denied. Teaching your children to have a respectful voice and set healthy boundaries will assist them in not being emotionally manipulated in their future.

In the work place, dismissal behavior will show up when there is an office project which has a specific deadline. The supervisor comes to you and says, *"I have such a heavy schedule this week, but I know you could do this project with your eyes closed."* Then, you finally agree, even though you are swamped yourself. You repeatedly request pertinent information from your supervisor in order to meet the deadline. The supervisor keeps dismissing you by making excuses, and doesn't provide the necessary information. Finally, the deadline is upon you and passes. The supervisor then blames you for not completing the project. He is upset at you that the department does not meet the expectations of the company. You are left feeling stunned and angry. You feel a sense of injustice rising up within you. Trapped again!

Living with, or being connected to, a passive-aggressive slowly destroys your self-worth and identity. I have had clients say, *"I just want to run away."* Still, others share when they are away from the passive-aggressive person, they feel free. Inner turmoil begins when knowing it's time to go home, attend a family function or go to work. If you are married or have a significant other, you may have tried to save the relationship. As Christian women, the messages in your mind might say something like, *"I just need to try harder to have a happy home. I need to be a good witness at work. I need to be more loving to my friend."* The guilty thoughts can smother you when they become distorted in faith-based communities. Over time, I have heard countless women say, *"I have slowly relinquished my heart and soul. I feel dead inside. I do not know what to believe any-more!"* This is all a result of the dismissal game.

When these thoughts become more frequent, you are becoming someone even you do not recognize. Often, women begin to feel they are not themselves. They report feeling and acting like the Wicked Witch of the West. Generally, this occurs when passive aggression has surfaced in their life and they feel it came out of the blue. Then, they ask, *"Lord, how did I get to this place and do I have to keep living with this thorn in my flesh?"* I know some of you are saying, *"Yes, Lord, that is exactly what I have asked myself many times."* The feelings of being trapped and waves of hopelessness may begin to overtake you. It is time to come out of your bondage and stop the generational cycle. Ladies, you are the apple of your heavenly Father's eye and He would not want you to become anybody other than how He created you; as a unique and gifted women. At times, it is hard to hold onto truth when you are in the midst of various hurtful chaotic situations. There is one other hallmark pattern used by passive-aggressive people. I refer to this pattern as "**Flipping the Script**", and it can create a crazy-making cycle. Therefore, having supportive, accountable and safe people in your life, who validate and speak truth about your situation is vital. Sisters, do not walk this journey alone.

FLIPPING THE SCRIPT ~ CRAZY-MAKING CYCLE

One of the cycles women encounter in passive-aggressive relationships is called *"Flipping the Script."* When you are in the center of a flip, one minute the environment is quite peaceful and lovable. The next minute, negative emotional chaos rocks the woman's world. For example, a woman may share about her busy week. The spouse seems to be listening and offering a couple of empathetic responses. The man appears to understand about the busy schedule. He remains attentive and engaged in the conversation. She feels heard as she explains the overload of dealing with the children's various activities. She continues to share that this has also been an unusual work week. Later on in the conversation, she communicates that his working extra hours has put additional stress on her during this unusually hectic week. All of a sudden with one swift unexpected shift a flip happens.

The passive-aggressive person reacts with statements such as, *"It sounds like you have not organized yourself very well. If you had been on top of things this week, it would not have been so hectic. I don't understand what was so hard."* The woman is dumbfounded. She was feeling a level of closeness, safety and intimacy. Wham! She is now puzzled and uncertain about what just happened. The personal attack comes in passive and aggressive ways. As soon as the woman made a reference about the man's schedule adding to her stress, the script was flipped. So what happened? The passive-aggressor heard what she stated as a personal attack. All empathy and listening stopped and was replaced by critical judgment and blame. Flipping the script occurs when someone includes insinuation, blame, anger, irritation or responses with sarcastic reactions.

The above scenario gives a picture of a **"Flipping the Script"** relational pattern where things seem to be calm and then change in a heartbeat. The passive-aggressive person lacks the willingness to acknowledge facts because they feel personally attacked. This is directly related to them experiencing inner turmoil. The inner turmoil leads to an automatic protective measure in the form of flipping the script; so he doesn't feel responsible for any part of the problem. Over time, this crazy-making communication style becomes habitual. Ladies, when the man came back at her, one of the ways she could have responded would have been to use the "XYZW" tool. The components of this tool are as follows:

- When you said **X**
- I heard or I felt **Y**
- What I would like or request from you is **Z**
- Will you do it? That final question is the **W**. This is usually the step women leave out. If you do not complete this step, it will be a matter of time and the P-A will renege on their agreements. Usually, using the tactic of ***"selective memory"*** by saying *"Oh, I forgot or I never said I would agree."*

~ WALLS of DETACHMENT ~

Ladies, these types of scenarios can be very frustrating. They lead women to begin building protective barriers. Over time, these barriers create *emotional walls of detachment* to prevent further hurt and pain. There is a distinct feeling that you are somehow losing your personhood. After a period of time, you may develop physical signs of distress such as, headaches, muscle aches and irritable stomach patterns. Wishing and hoping for a change in someone is an empty goal. Whenever there are negative feelings unexpressed or not dealt with in a healthy, constructive way, eventually they will poison relationships. **My sisters, you can not wait for the person to change, you must step out of these mind games and receive your own healing**. However, it is okay to pray for, healthy, intimate and connected relationships. I repeat, if you need help, seek it as soon as possible. Reaching out and bringing a halt to the silence may include counseling, coaching, accountability partners, and supportive group process.

Passive-aggressive men have communicated to me, that certain events impact them. They sense a need to defend themselves and their actions. These mind-gymnastics pivot from a ***"trigger key"*** for them. Situations which trigger or activate feelings of powerlessness, fear or insecurity will kick in passive-aggressive behaviors. To the receivers of these behaviors, it will appear out of nowhere. However, when you begin to see the protective measures he is taking, you will also be less blind-sided because you will know when he attempts to flip the script. Sometimes, women begin to feel responsible for the flip of the script and they begin to try hard to fix the problem. Ladies, this is an example of how you become ensnared in the P-A dance. **People get irritated, but with the passive-aggressive person, irritation, harsh tone of voice, minimizing concerns or blaming are classic characteristics**. Questions are heard as a potential threat or a personal attack. Undoubtedly, these are crazy-making patterns. It becomes difficult to get support from others because they cannot see the whole process.

Women, who are married to men in leadership within the church, shared with me that they are filled with guilt and shame. Christian women in passive-aggressive relationships communicate they often feel like they are living a double life. Frequently, at home the passive-aggressive person is full of rage and sabotages their relationship. Then, this same person might go to church, praising God, then comes home and uses the silent treatment. Nothing is said to the woman as to why he is silent. Little does she know it was instituted to reinforce some form of displeasure, yet, it is not directly communicated to the woman. After repetitive scenarios, women start building a wall, brick by brick. In an attempt to keep out the hurt, women also keep out the good. Other women stated the men in their lives would defer to them, by not accepting responsibility. Letting their wives take the leadership role in the relationship. What a cycle! Do you see yourself in this type of scenario? What have you been doing to deal with this cycle?

Denial of the chaos is a pathway to doubt and frustration. Most women know they are experiencing subtle attacks, but never understand the reasons. Unlike domestic violators, there are no out-ward injuries or scars when dealing with passive aggression. Women discuss how the emotional and verbal putdowns are vague enough to create self-doubt. One of the communication patterns of the passive aggressive person is to function like a **strike force**. They will get verbal digs in, and then disappear while leaving the victim thinking, *"Where did that drama come from, or what in the world was that response all about?"* One of the reasons the passive-aggressive person does this ***strike force*** tactic is to throw you off balance.

People, who turn out to be aggressive, will often become verbally abusive depending on how threatened they feel during an interaction. Unlike domestic violence, the verbal abuse of a passive-aggressive person is often done to silence you, rather than physically injure or kill. The **strike force** tactic is used to prevent others from exposing their inadequacies, insecurities or fears. They will attempt to stop an argument or questions by using an intimidating tone of voice. The behavioral pattern is similar to a rattlesnake who warns you to back off and leave them alone; otherwise, they will strike out. This can be deadly, because emotional and verbal abuse kills the spirit and soul of a person. Do you have suppressed feelings or resentments which may be causing you emotional, spiritual or physical problems? If so, see if you can track it down to get to the root issue.

Abuse behaviors are extremely destructive and wound the heart and personhood of a person. However, the Lord did not create women to be dangled like puppets; nor to become manipulated or controlled by others. The Lord not only sees you, but He sees the person wounding you and He will deal justly with all people who harm His sons and daughters. The Lord loves the passive-aggressive person and stands ready to enter into their redemptive and healing journey. There are certain areas which will be dealt with as the person walks the process of recovery healing. The healing work the passive-aggressive person has to accomplish includes:

- Taking responsibility for reactionary actions.
- Admit what they are doing is not working relationally.

- Take the steps to regain balance, renew attitudes and correct distorted mindsets.
- Identify core roots of anger and resentments that promote hostile behavior.
- Identify reasons for their *"get-even with others"* tactics, when they sense personal injustice.
- Give self permission to relax and be vulnerable to share honestly.
- Learn to feel good about personal identity.
- Learn to speak up without becoming defensive.
- Acknowledge and heal family system influences.
- Obtain and implement healthy communication and conflict resolution tools.
- Learn to be a person of integrity.
- Learn to forgive self and others.

*Power Tool: "*Dear ones, you must stand up, straighten your back, hold your head up high and walk in victory and freedom. Be strong, bold and courageous! Do not be afraid or terrified. The Lord promises to be with you and He will never leave or abandon you.*"

PICKING UP THE TOOLS ~ PUTTING INTO PRACTICE

Awareness of passive aggressive tendencies and defensive patterns will enable women to make healthy decisions concerning relationships. In Proverbs 4:5 the word says, "*Get wisdom and understanding.*" The promise we can claim is that, we do not need to lack knowledge. **In this next section, I am including some practical tools you can use and a sample of how to state what you need to voice**. Before you proceed, let me warn you, when confronting or setting boundaries, get ready to experience the following behaviors: pouting, silent treatment, minimizing, denial, blame and detouring. I realize, to some, the tools and action step may seem harsh. I assure you, it is necessary when communicating with passive aggressive people. Yes, you will feel some inner turmoil, until you have integrated the tools.

- **Yes, No, Maybe So**: The P-A (passive-aggressive) has difficulty actually stating what they want. Although, when you encourage them to share, they feel they have communicated their needs, and so why repeat themselves. Many women, I have seen in my practice, feel this type of P-A man is maddening. Remember, the P-A man does not express his resentment or hostility openly. Rather, it is hidden under a facade of "Niceness" which presents a boyish naivety and passivity.

  Tool: Learn to repeat what you heard them say. This is not psycho babble, you really need to repeat and then write out what you heard. If you really want something done in a specific time frame, state it and share action you will take if incomplete. Write down what has been agreed upon. P-A people are known for denying what they said. They run from you thinking they have committed to something. They try to leave a loophole open. Ladies close the loop holes!

  Taking Action: When communicating be sure to repeat what you heard the person state. *"Are you telling me that you will get the car emission test? The deadline is this Friday. If you are not able to commit to the deadline, please let me know now and I will get the test done today. Ok, so we agree you will take the car for the emission test."*

- **Invalidating and Disregard**: Consistent refusal to take ownership or acknowledge the realities of life. Women have shared, the P-A men in their lives will make statements similar to, *"I never said that"* or *"Why are you saying that, I don't know what you are talking about."*

  Tool: Do not engage in a power struggle. Once you are pulled into a power struggle and become reactive, you have walked head-on into the *"P-A's world of the crazies."*

  Take Action: *"I know you think you did not state _____, though this is what I heard. However, if you do not remember, let's revisit the situation and I will write it down so we both have a record of what we talked about for future reference."*

- **Minimizing**: If a P-A feels you are going to confront them on their beliefs or statements, they will counterattack by making minimizing comments such as: *"You're way too sensitive"* or *"You're exaggerating"* or *"You are making a big deal out of nothing."* Then, if you confront the underline anger in an attempt to get to the root of issues, aggression may show up in a harsh tone and tensed body language. The purpose of this aggressive stance is to shut you up or shut you down, thereby avoiding direct confrontation. The P-A counts on you not wanting to get into a big messy argument and so you will see the show of aggression, like a cobra hissing. When a cobra hisses it means **"Back off right now!"** Guess what ladies? I know most of you back off and the P-A feels they have won. They then learn from you, how to treat you. If you allow this tactic to continue to be successful, the person learns that a show of aggression will cause you to back off.

  Tool: Ladies, you are not to be tolerated or de-valued. You are a daughter of the King of Kings. You are worthy to be treated with honor. When you see or hear posturing or tones of aggression, address it immediately. There is a difference between being irritable and raising your voice versus expressing aggression and intimidation.

  Taking Action: One of the ways you can respond, is to use is the **"XYZW"** tool.

The components of this tool are as follows:

1. When you say/do X
2. I heard or I felt Y
3. What I would like from you or request is Z
4. Will you do it is the W (This is usually the step women leave out. If you do not complete this step, it will be a matter of time and the P-A person will renege. Often, using the tactic of **"selective memory"**, by saying, **"Oh I forgot."**

~ Set aside a few minutes, choose a situation and fill in the blanks ~

Practice using the "XYZW" tool: *"When you say/do _____, I feel/hear _____. What I want/request is _____. Will you do it?_____. It is important to get that agreement; otherwise there is no accountability for the future. This way you have a baseline to refer back to: "The last time we talked about this, you agreed to_____. What has changed, that you are not following through?"*

- **Feelings Attacked**: When you share you have been wounded by the P-A and you nail the truth, he will protest that he did nothing wrong. Claiming and believing they have been victimized by others, allows the P-A to excuse owning his own behaviors. The view and opinion of others outside the home is crucial to the intricate belief system the P-A sets up in his mind. The hope is that outside people, will feel he is the victim of your requests of him. This is a ploy to protect them.

    Tool: Take responsibility for your own actions. However, acknowledge open antagonism of the P-A person. Ladies, I have a warning to share. You must know your needs and desires in order to communicate effectively. Avoid generalities and steer away from speaking in an aggressive manner. **However, be assertive and consistent in maintaining your boundaries**. Communicate directly and clearly that you will not be disrespected. Be clear about addressing the particular patterns or cycles that are disturbing to you. My sisters, boundaries that you are not willing to follow through with will not work. If appropriate, you can use the tool of offering options and he can select one.

    Taking Action: For example: *"I realize, we have not been able to agree on a color for the paint. I will get some more color schemes and I will select three. Anyone of the three you choose will be fine with me."*

***Power Tool**: "*I can not stress more the importance of consistently implementing all tools which relate to your situation. **Do not give up if it doesn't work out well the first time**. Record what did and did not work. Expect to feel internal resistance, as you practice and make your tools fit your own personality style. Whenever people step out of toxic or unhealthy cycles, the other person will not accept you changing the familiar patterns. So, they will respond many times in defensive or dismissing ways. The hope is you will not try again. I encourage you to keep going until the cycles are broken and you are able to step out of the "passive-aggressive dance."*

~ Prayer ~

"*My Abba Father, Jehovah Jireh, I pray that you provide the wisdom and courage to help me stand strong. I am searching for you with all my heart. I am so glad you are trustworthy and faithful. I trust you with my feelings and my hurts. I am thankful you are helping me to stop denying the realities of my life. You have said if I seek you, I would find you. I ask you to pour out your peace and grace daily in my life. Today, I choose to give you the hurt places of my heart, so I will soar freely like an eagle above the raging storms. Amen.*"

Chapter 6

Identifying Origins ~
Patterns from Past Pain

"Surely you desire honesty from the womb,
teaching me wisdom even there." (Psalm 51:6)

Dealing with a passive-aggressive person is challenging, but understanding the origin of this personality style brings clarity. It answers how they became so hurt, and why they hurt others. It's difficult to understand why someone can appear so nice one minute and so mean another minute. **Ladies, as you receive understanding concerning the origin of these behaviors, the frustration and disillusionment fades away.** Knowing the root causes of passive aggression will help to answer why having a decent conversation is so challenging. Understanding the origin also brings clarity of how someone can seemingly switch personalities so quickly. It answers the question as to how the passive-aggressive personality blind-sides you, and why the emotional chaos continues. These scenarios are not unique to you. They have been pondered and analyzed by many women who attempt to make some semblance of stability in the chaos.

We are all influenced by our environments. People who have gone before us do affect us generationally. It is important to understand the prevailing culture, regardless of whether it is the culture at home, work, church or significant relationships. Some adults grew up in homes where they received guidance and support. These homes modeled by word and deed how to live in a healthy way. The talk matched the walk. Not perfect, but real in owning their weaknesses and celebrating the whole person. However, if you did not have some of these ingredients in place, then a negative legacy will follow. Often, it begs the question, "Why didn't someone have my back." I want to encourage you by saying, it is not too late. The Lord desires to have everything in the light. All you uncover and put into the light will bring you closer to freedom, and further from shame and doubt. The passive-aggressive person has unresolved rage from their childhood and is experiencing an internal dialogue. There is a desire for intimacy, but it's sabotaged by periods of covert anger and progressive rage.

The childhood need for love and affirmation produces the passive side of the person. Unmet needs from significant people in the passive-aggressive person's past makes it difficult to be too vulnerable. It is a risk for them to express too much rage, although it is always percolating just below the surface and felt by those close to them. The unexpressed hurt, emotional neglect, shame, verbal cruelty and emotional ridicule produces the aggressive patterns, attitudes and behavior.

Ladies, you must realize you are not responsible for creating the characteristics of the passive-aggressive person. The good news is you both have a healer and a redeemer waiting for you to call on Him. God, also known as Jehovah Rapha, can heal you and the passive-aggressive person. Yes, it is difficult to conceive, but God loves you and He loves the passive-aggressor. God knows exactly what happened in our past and if we pursue restoration, our Heavenly Father will step in and divinely intervene. He will restore the passive-aggressive person to wholeness if they seek help. In Jeremiah this precept is revealed and confirmed stating, *"O Lord, if you heal me, I will be truly healed . . ." (Jeremiah 17:14)*

TOXIC ENVIRONMENTS ~
FERTILE BREEDING GROUND

Abuse in any form affects the entire family; crosses all societal, racial, religious and economic lines. It undermines a person's value by seeking to control, manipulate and dominate others. Abuse will escalate in intensity and frequency if not dealt with proactively. It's no secret that the past affects the present and future. With that in mind, you understand that even as adults, the childhood experiences have bearing on actions and reactions. Children protect themselves the only way they knew how at the time. However, so often they carry the same protective behaviors into adulthood. The survival skills they utilized are no longer working to keep them feeling secure and "normal." Even though it may be difficult to read the following lists, it's essential you understand how various environments create dysfunctional cycles. A dysfunctional family is a family where conflict, destructive behaviors, and often abuse of members occur continually and regularly, leading to accommodating actions. The people in the family function with the understanding that the patterns are normal. Only in extreme cases would a majority of the list be present, however, any combination and single item can create dysfunctional cycles.

Emotionally Disconnected &Abusive Environments:
- Children were not permitted to make their own choices.
- Projection and transfer of blame was put upon the child or adolescent.
- Alterations of reality such as, "Dad is not drunk, he is only tired."
- Overprotecting, smothering, excusing and blaming others as a common pattern of the family.
- Decreasing self worth and self esteem through high or even non-existent expectations.
- Refusal to discuss abusive behaviors in the home.
- Not allowed to express true emotions, or punishment for openly expressing emotions.
- Spoken or unspoken rules, to keep family secrets.

Relationally Uninvolved Environments:
- Parents, or caregiver, failed to love and nurture the child.
- Permissive environment had no structure or boundaries.
- Child was not listened to, heard or believed.
- Child is expected to provide emotional nurturing to the parents, to make them feel good.
- Parental figures are not emotionally or physically present.
- Failure to encourage education or intellectual development.
- Shamed due to learning and social challenges such as, learning disabilities, ADD, or ADHD
- Teased and felt different than other children.

Physically Distracted /Neglectful Environment:
- Lack of food, clothes, shelter may have led to embarrassment.
- Left alone when it was not age-appropriate.
- Failure to provide medical or dental care.
- Allowing, or encouraging the use of, drugs and alcohol.
- Parental use of drugs or alcohol.
- Failure to protect from the abuse of others.

Verbally Cruel Environment:
- Excessive guilt-making behavior of blaming and shaming.
- Name-calling, put-downs, sarcasm, and comparisons.
- Teasing, laughing at, instead of with the person, or being belittled.
- Deliberate deception, including mind games.
- Bombarding with questions and verbally punishing if not answering quickly.
- Constantly verbalizing critical comments about others in, and outside, the family.

Physically Violent Environment:
- Slapping, shaking, scratching, squeezing, hitting, and beating with objects such as boards, sticks, belts, kitchen utensils, electric cords or shovels.
- Throwing, pushing, shoving, and slamming against walls or objects.
- Threatening with perceived or real intent to hurt and harm.
- Forcing of food or water, or starvation of child.

Sexually Abusive Environment:
- Fondling, inappropriate touching, or exposing self.
- Having sex or committing sexual acts with the child or adolescent.
- No teaching about sex, puberty or menstruation.
- Discrimination due to gender.
- Flirtation or sexually degrading behaviors.

When a person grows up in toxic environments, they experience trauma and pain from significant others or parents. The trauma and pain may come through actions, words and attitudes. When this occurs, a person grows up changed, feeling different, missing important parts of necessary parenting that prepare them for adulthood. Children will learn to grow-up hiding or separating their feelings by developing survival roles to cope with stress and dysfunctional relationships. Some people grow up with inner anxiety and rage, yet do not know why they feel the way they do. Passive aggressors have toxic shame-based belief systems.

Beliefs systems can be an influential source or our worst nightmare. Our belief system consists of our core values, which we base the things we do, say or believe in to function in our daily lives. As part of the healing process, we must evaluate the truth of our belief system. A shame-based person develops a protective filter which prevents positive or complimentary messages from being received. **Shame releases internal messages such as:**

- *"You are not worthy,"* which told the child they were bad as a person. "I am bad regardless of what I do, even if my actions are good." This message leads to immobilizing patterns. For instance; the person will show an inability to complete projects, out of fear of failing. They may also believe, they can not meet other people's expectations.
- *"You are not good enough,"* which told the child they would be acceptable if they would do more to get people's approval. This message leads to perfectionism and performance patterns.
- *"You don't belong,"* which told the child they are not part of the family, because they were different in an unacceptable way. This

message leads to withdrawal whenever feelings are exposed or the person feels vulnerable.

- ***"You are unlovable,"*** which told the child they are not worthy of being loved. They grow up thinking they cannot be loved. This message may lead to judgmental and critical beliefs of self and others.

Another outcome of growing up in toxic or unhealthy environments is adopting distorted roles. Our roles in a family aren't just about our age, gender, or birth order. It can have a lot to do with the identity we develop to fit our family style. It is impossible to identify passive-aggressive traits and tendencies without discussing the dynamics of toxic family system roles. Typically, the family members of these systems do what they can to bring consistency, safety and some form of structure to a system that is becoming emotionally disconnected, unpredictable, chaotic or frightening. In order to make sure this happens, members fall into certain roles or a mixture of roles which serves to meet needs of the family. These roles maintain a distorted level of loyalty which is frequently stronger than individual needs.

Each member in a toxic family will perform a certain role to allow the family as a whole to survive. Yet, most needs go unmet in toxic families. Let's identify some of the main family roles. *Roles can dictate the way shame may manifest itself in a person's adult years.* It is important to note that it is possible to be healed, transformed, and delivered by the redemptive internal work of the Holy Spirit. What was once toxic or destructive can be redeemed and freedom can be experienced. Amen!

~ ROLES OF TOXIC or UNHEALTHY FAMILY SYSTEMS ~

The Family Champion is often old before their time. This person tries to always do what is right and is known as super responsible. This child usually takes over the role of a parent at a young age, becoming self-sufficient and very responsible. There is a tendency to work very hard for approval from other people. The responsible role may be a high achiever, but what they really desire from their family is for the family to be proud of them. Inside they may feel lonely, hurt, confused, angry, and fearful. Some people in the family may have referred to this person as the "little man" or "little mama."

- **Without Restoration:** As an adult the family champion may become a workaholic; have difficulty in admitting they are wrong; feel responsible for everything, be hard-working, marries or dates a dependent personality, such as an alcoholic, perfectionist, or a person with low self-esteem. They have a hard time saying no and setting healthy boundaries. Frequently, they believe they can't fail because of what it would do to the family name. Men who take on a super-responsible role may become a passive-aggressive person.
- **Distorted Beliefs:** *"If I do not take care of it, no one will."* Another belief of a family champion will be, "If I do not do this, something horrible will happen or things will deteriorate." This person thinks and believes, "I must stay in control of my feelings at all times."
- **With Restoration:** Part of the restorative process is to learn to accept potential failures and shortcomings by taking responsibility for their own actions.
- **Redemptive work of the Holy Spirit:** The family champion is a great executive and manager. The person's strengths are: Goal-oriented, decisive, self-disciplined, leadership abilities, very competent, organized, successful, and an initiator. Additionally, they make wonderful leaders, visionaries and pioneers of new work because they love diversity and variety.

The Problem Kid is often seeking attention at any price. They may also be known as the scapegoat or rebel child. This person is angry, defiant, negative and looking for attention and approval. The family feels most ashamed of the acting out rebel child. The person will compete with everyone in the family, except the family champion. Yet, this child is the most emotionally honest child in the family. They act out the stress, tension, fears, and anger, the family has a tendency to ignore or minimize. There may be many harmful behaviors in the family such as alcoholism. It does not matter whether the attention is negative or positive. The child's role is to provide a distraction from the real issues in the family. These children are usually the most sensitive and caring, which is why they feel tremendous hurt and pain. They are romantics, but remain cynical and distrustful. The rebel has felt unloved by family members and parents. They usually are the first person to get into a restorative place due to the result of their destructive behaviors.

- **Without Restoration:** Often times the females have a *"father hunger"* and may connect with unhealthy males to fill a hole in the heart. This could result in unplanned pregnancy. They are known as the troublemaker in school and at work. Males may end up in prison or develop alcoholism, drug dependencies, frequent job loss, experience extreme truancy or legal problems.
- **Distorted Beliefs:** The thought, *"If I scream loudly enough, somebody is bound to hear and see me."* They also think it is fine to, *"Take whatever you need, because you cannot count on anybody anyway."* The rebel feels angry most of the time, but doesn't know why.
- **With Restoration:** The restorative process for the rebel will require them to accept responsibility, while developing an identity. They will need to learn how to have courage and gain the ability to function under pressure or stress. Mentors can assist in helping them stay focused during their healing process.
- **Redemptive work of the Holy Spirit:** Make wonderful addiction counselors, youth workers and leadership trainers. The person's strengths involve creativity, honesty, sense of humor, and an ability to lead. They are risk takers.

The Lost Child never wants to make waves and in essence, becomes invisible. This child escapes by attempting to be overlooked. They are daydreamers who are often ignored. They grow up in their own fantasized world, by reading a lot of books, watching a lot of television or becoming compulsive with computers. They deal with reality by withdrawing or rationalizing any hurtful, fearful or emotionally threatening events. They will often become an adjuster, with buried hostility. This person grows up being named the "quiet, shy or sensitive one." As adults they find themselves unable to be honest, and feel low self-worth. They become terrified of intimacy and will sabotage any relationship which might potentially expose their insecurities. Without healing they are socially isolated in order to prevent being hurt. The lost adult will count on others to give them a voice. Many times the family doesn't miss this *"Lost Child"* for days. They have a tendency to drift and float through life. Often, they become athletes so they can hide out and yet receive affirmation at the same time.

- **Without Restoration:** They have little zest for life and do not set many goals. They may have sexual identity problems and become promiscuous. Often, the lost child dies at an early age because of experimentation with alcohol and drugs. As an adult, this person seldom relaxes even when having fun. They may suffer from headaches, stomach problems, and anxiety. This person has a very difficult time saying no and may have a great deal of false guilt. They struggle, because they are afraid of what people might think about them. The "Lost Child" has rigid internal rules and usually becomes passive-aggressive in relationships of those they perceive have more authority or may expose inadequacies. They have fear and difficulty perceiving options and choices. This adult hates change and functions best having rigid routines. The person may have trouble making decisions. Many times these adults function with fears which prevent healthy intimate relationships from developing. However, they crave approval; therefore they will volunteer for anything they are asked to do, to serve others.
- **Distorted Beliefs:** The "Lost Child" role believes, *"If I am nice, then people will like me."* Another thought is, *"If I focus on others, then maybe people won't notice me."*
- **With Restoration:** They enjoy staying in the background, so they do not bring any attention to themselves. However, with restoration they learn to find and use their voice.
- **Redemptive work of the Holy Spirit:** When the "Lost Child" becomes a healed adult, they make wonderful servant heart

people in assisting others to fulfill their destinies. The strengths of this adult include being flexible, quiet, talented, and creative and generally have an ability to be a healthy follower.

The Stress Reliever, also known as the **family clown**, is a laugh a minute while feelings are being stuffed inside. They tend to be cute, anxious, hyper, immature, and will generally do anything for a chuckle. There is a tendency to feel insecure, inadequate, fearful and confused. They are usually called the life of the party, but are not having fun on the inside. This child takes ownership for the emotional well-being of the family. They become the family's social director and comic relief by diverting the family's attention from the anger and pain. Their identity is centered on others. They do not know how to get their needs met. The stress reliever personality becomes an adult who cannot receive love, only give it. They often have trophies of people they have helped rather than true friendships. This family role may connect themselves to abusive, unhealthy, and unstable people in order to "save" them. They have short attention spans and therefore may be poor students. Often we see them as people-pleasers.

- **Without Restoration:** The stress reliever has a tendency to develop ulcers because they can't handle stress and usually internalize their hurts. They can be compulsive and usually marry or connect themselves to people who grew-up in the family champion role. Women can become secret drinkers or have other dependencies. They may appear to be on the verge of hysterics. Stress reliever females may be known as "Drama Queens."
- **Distorted Beliefs:** The stress releiver's self-talk, says things like, *"If I can make people laugh, there will be no pain or hurt. I can stop the pain for awhile."*
- **With Restoration:** This person must learn to take care of self and to be serious when appropriate. It's a major part of the restorative process to become self-controlled.
- **Redemptive work of the Holy Spirit:** The redeemed family stress reliever is fabulous at jobs or ministries which require great people skills. They make charming host or hostesses.

The child becomes an adult who is valued for their kind heart, and generosity, as they learn to listen to others. This person's strengths include people connections because they are fun to be with and have a great sense of humor. They are also able to relieve stress and pain with a quick wit and independent spirit. After the redemptive work of the Holy Spirit, they may become wonderful teachers and great story tellers of truth.

The Chief Enabler is also known as a protector who keeps things the same. This role is a person who is the nurturer of the family system. This child is usually the closest emotionally to the unhealthy parent or significant other in the family. Frequently, this role is filled by a daughter. If it is a son, this child is constantly attempting to protect the mother. However, as an adult the enabler will have a great deal of resentments towards both parents. The enabler becomes responsible for everyone in the family who needs help to survive. They are known as the martyr, protector, rescuer, excuser and charmer. This person lives with a lot of self imposed guilt or denial when things do not turn out okay for the family.

- **Without Restoration:** The enabler will develop a low self-esteem because the family is not functioning well and they blame themselves for the outcome. They have a hard time trusting, so their relationships often end up broken or in divorce. Over time this person may deal with chronic depression. The enabler may have control issues trying to prevent people from experiencing consequences of actions. Internally they may feel powerless, helpless, angry and inadequate because they fear their reality will not change, no matter what they try.
- **Distorted Beliefs:** They may think and believe, *"If I take care of you, you won't leave or reject me"* or *"I have to take care of other people's feelings."* Others believe, *"I can't let this happen."*
- **With Restoration**: The Protector, enabler, will become increasingly confident. They learn to do self-care and set healthy boundaries without false guilt. They will confront with assertive skills rather than being conflict avoiders.

- **Redemptive work of the Holy Spirit**: The restored enabler has a great deal of mercy. Their strengths include sensitivity, compassion, and grace. They are empathic listeners who are wonderfully loyal friends. The healthy enabler personality is able to be a wonderful mentor. They will also do well in a variety of people-oriented jobs which involve serving, such as, the medical arena.

Adults, who come from a childhood of traumatic environments, develop certain protective roles. Additionally, they may develop abusive patterns or negative behaviors of their own. The young child who develops a passive-aggressive personality had their tender spirits crushed. The Abba Father acknowledges this truth. Proverbs 15:13 reinforces this psychological fact by stating, *"A glad heart makes a happy face; a broken heart crushes the spirit."* If someone else in the family experienced abuse; the affect this has on a person is often as severe as if it had happened personally. The cycles of abuse will continue if there is no ownership of the events or personal healing. The person and their offspring are in danger of repeating the passive aggressive or violent behaviors.

Many children, who experienced various forms of negativity, become the kind of parents who scream at their own children. If they never saw a balanced method of dealing with hurt, anger, disappointment, loss and injustice, they will not know how to cope with the challenges associated with raising a family. Passive-aggressive people are easily frustrated when things do not go their way.

No family has it all together. We all live with some form of dysfunction. The perception, and meaning, a child gives an event is often more powerful than the event itself. That being said, there are certain environments which may lead to specific beliefs, behaviors and unhealthy patterns. When a child grows up in certain family scenarios, there is an impact on them as an adult, which must be addressed, so the patterns do not continue to be perpetuated in the next generations. Many children who grew up in unhealthy households of alcoholism, addiction, incest, abuse, or with a chronically ill parent *(physical, depression, or other mental illness)* develop an increased propensity to live out similar patterns. When people deny the reality of their upbringing, or place the circumstances on a shelf and believe they were not impacted, they find the impact pops up at some point in their adult life. In the next chapter we will look at the behaviors, and cycles which need to be broken.

~ Prayer ~

"Lord, thank you for opening my eyes to the truth. I pray for more understanding. I am grateful for your faithfulness. Amen."

Chapter 7

Tendencies and Traits ~

Unhealthy Family Systems

"I love your sanctuary, Lord, the place where your glorious presence dwells." (Psalm 26:8)

Incidents from family systems can influence current attitudes and behaviors. The following characteristics may be exhibited in adult children from alcoholic, unhealthy, or toxic family systems. These characteristics may be observed primarily in families who engage in denial, abuse, rage or domestic violence. Children who were raised in families with a chronically ill or a depressed parent, helplessness, permissiveness, or emotional disconnection will also exhibit the following characteristics. Take a look at the described characteristics of a destructive or unhealthy family system. As you do, see if you identify any patterns within your current life, or maybe your own childhood family system. How many of the following characteristics does the passive-aggressive person you are dealing with possess?

- **Fear of Trusting:** Children in family systems that were unpredictable and where adults were unresponsive to their needs, have trouble trusting other people. Also, children who grew up relying on themselves for self-care rather than on adults, learn not to trust or ask for help. They also learn not to need or show vulnerability. They fear becoming too close or seeking intimacy with others, because they may be rejected, betrayed or abandoned.

- **Pervasive Sense of Guilt:** Often, children from toxic or unhealthy systems grow up with a sense of helplessness or self-judgment. Frequently, these children try to make sense of the pain in their lives. These children tend to believe they caused the responses and behaviors of others. Instead of feeling like a victim, they falsely assume they are responsible for the drama and trauma in their environment. Soon, beliefs such as, *"It's my fault that mom was depressed. If I was only better at...."* As adults, they live with a pervasive sense of guilt even when they have done nothing wrong. So whenever a person asks questions which appear potentially exposing, they become defensive.

- **Hyper-Responsible or Chronically Irresponsible:** Children will become hyper-responsible in response to their environments. They are pretty black and white reactors. There were no grey areas. Many children became people pleasers. Trying to please their parents by doing more or trying harder. Others came to an understanding that it did not make any difference. This *"what's the point"* thinking persists into adulthood. The belief system is that their actions determine other people's behavior. This belief may lead some to feel that nothing they do will be good enough.

- **Perfectionist Behavior:** Adult children who learned to *"walk on egg shells"* feared being perceived as doing something wrong. Each time they attempted to meet the expectations of others, the bar was raised and thus they could never attain approval. As adults they can become approval seekers, critical or perfectionist. Perfectionists are sticklers for doing things right, becoming performance based in relationships. Some adults have difficulty giving themselves the okay to make mistakes. They judge others through black and white standards, a lens of good and bad.

- **Need to be in Control:** If a child grew up not knowing what to expect, the need to control is intensified. Calm seasons that mix with eruptions of chaos create insecurity and instability for children. These children grow up repeating this same pattern as adults.

- **Difficulty Hearing Positives:** Due to a poor self-image developed in childhood, adult children either discount positive feedback or feel a sense of distrust, which feeds the feeling of pain or loss. The adults learn to dismiss, or quickly minimize, other's feedback. The inability to receive positives leads to emptiness.

- **Dependence and Fear of Dependency:** The attitude develops early in life that, *"I have, or shouldn't have needs. I can do it myself, thank you very much."* When needs are repeatedly not met or others aren't emotionally, physically, or spiritually available, children learn to stop needing. In fact, may fear times of a healthy and balanced relational connection as adults. Thus, developing vulnerable and intimate relationships may be a struggle for them and their significant partners.

- **Secrecy:** They believe they must constantly live up to the beliefs held up to them in childhood. There are also secrets which create an inability to openly communicate. Usually there is a family member who becomes the "pain" holder. Unspoken and spoken harsh rules persist into adulthood: don't talk; don't trust; don't feel; don't resolve; don't acknowledge a mistake; and don't accept reality.

- **Over or Under Achievement:** Living in a legalistic, black-and-white world, these adult children often develop patterns in trying to gain self-esteem from the outside world. There is an attempt to seek praise in place of love, or to isolate themselves out of fears and exposure of inadequacies. Some adults may even develop substance abuse and compulsive patterns.

- **Need to be Right:** Often the need to be correct replaces an original desire to be loved. Unable to admit when they are wrong, they very rarely apologize unless the other person takes the initiative to say they are sorry. The passive-aggressive person believes their inner turmoil is caused by others, and so they very rarely apologize or seek forgiveness. Eventually, they stop doing common courtesies, such as, *"please, thank you or excuse me."*

- **Fear of Feelings:** Expressing feelings was not a safe form of communication in the child's family system. Children were often only permitted certain emotions that brought calm to the home or agreed with parental emotions at the time. When unacceptable feelings were expressed, the risk of emotional and relational abandonment from parents or significant others were just round the corner.

- **Fear of Conflict or Anger:** Due to fears of destructive anger or threat of violence experienced in childhood, they learned to numb out feelings until the ability to feel and express their anger was lost. Some adults who experienced this can cry but never allow personal feelings of anger. Others can allow anger but never risk showing emotions or tears.

- **Seeks approval and affirmation:** The message a child received was very puzzling. The love they did experience was usually uncertain. The messages were ambiguous and mixed. *"Frequently, they invite people to care, but they push away."* "Come here, go away. Very inconsistent. Some children grew up with some confusion about themselves. The affirmations given by others are interpreted as being either neutral or negative. Other times, they may have received, but were not permitted to give love back. The hole to be loved remains until adulthood. In an attempt to fill the hole, people may select unhealthy relationships, addictions or seek inappropriate approval.

- **Feels like an Outsider:** Feeling different is something a person has experienced since childhood. Even if the circumstance does not warrant it, the feeling prevails. They were never completely comfortable playing with other children, because, many times a child felt they were on the outside looking in. Concerns about home problems clouded everything else in life.

- **Extreme Loyalty***:* This person is expected to be extremely loyal, even when there's evidence the loyalty is not earned. The children in some families live under an unspoken, or spoken, rule to be very loyal no matter what is going on at home. This form of loyalty is more the result of fear, or family insecurity than anything else. Nonetheless, the behavior which was modeled is one where no one walks away just because the going gets rough. There is a tendency to stay too long in unhealthy relationships. It may also be difficult to confront unhealthy behaviors in relationships which lead to an avoidance pattern of passivity.

- **Half Truth Teller:** There was a lot of masquerading, hiding or covering up issues in the family. Denial of unpleasant realities, broken promises and inconsistencies occurs in some homes. Truth telling was difficult because if you shared what was really happening behind closed doors, it might be seen as being disloyal to the family system. Therefore, denial and keeping the secrets helped to maintain life in some sort of order. A way of surviving the realities. Survival skills are a powerful thing in this person's life.

- **Denies that their past existed or affected them in any significant way**. For example, this person may say, *"I grew up in an alcoholic family too, but it didn't affect me."* They have what is referred to as the **Emotional Circuit-Breaker Effect.** Circuit breakers are an essential safety device. Whenever electrical wiring has too much current flowing through it, the circuit breaker cuts the power off until someone can fix the problem. The circuit breaker is a solution to a potentially damaging problem. This is the same way a person turns on an emotional circuit breaker, when they feel an overload of hurtful emotions. Fearful, that they will be overwhelmed by the truth of their environments, they shut off the potential of an emotional flood. P-A people have developed the emotional circuit breaker skill.

Power Tool: *Dear Ones, I believe this is a good place to stop and pray. What is the Holy Spirit telling you? I suggest you have some paper or journal handy when you want to capture what the Holy Spirit is communicating to you.*

FAMILY RULES ~ MESSING with YOUR MIND

The complex system of a passive-aggressive person runs deep. They seek to control their environment, so as not to reveal their own insecurities and inadequacies. They willfully take stands against anyone who does not agree with them. They are masters at turning things around to make the other person feel responsible for their discomfort. Many of the feelings of inadequacy and insecurities stem from distorted messages they receive within a family system. Unspoken family rules maintain the disruptive belief to remain silent, no matter what; keep it under wraps.

Silence permits all kinds of uncomfortable situations to persist. Often, the silent reality, referred to by outsiders as having a *pink elephant* in the room that nobody mentions. As a young child, if there were unmentionable issues, those *pink elephants* remain into adulthood. It's something everyone knows and feels, but no one talks about. Thus, unhealthy patterns continue and hurts remain unhealed. *You may want to take time and jot down known elephants in your childhood and adult relationships.* Pink elephants have a tendency to lead to an abundance of unhealthy rules. These rules might exist and manifest on the job, in churches and in families.

- *Family Rule*: Don't feel because you are not "really hurt." Get over it!
- **Message**: *No one cares if you are hurting. It is not safe to let people see your pain.*

- *Family Rule*: Don't talk or betray the family. You might tell the family secrets.
- **Message**: *Your feelings and thoughts really do not count. Keep our family business to yourself.*

- *Family Rule*: Don't trust or you will be vulnerable and might get hurt.
- **Message**: *Grow up fast. You have to depend totally on yourself.*

- *Family Rule*: Don't ask, because no one will listen or give you a direct answer.
- **Message**: *"What is wrong with you? Don't you act like you know more than everybody else?"*

- *Family Rule*: Don't be yourself. Try to avoid attention or responsibility.
- **Message**: *"You aren't all that smart. You are bad, selfish, or stupid."*

- *Family Rule*: Don't make a decision.
- **Message**: *It might be wrong and you will look like a foul.*

- *Family Rule*: Don't resolve.
- **Message**: *You won't have to be responsible for the results.*

*Power Tool: *"Ladies, look back at childhood experiences in order to understand why you think and do what you do. Do not go back to blame. Otherwise, you may blame others for your struggles and battles, and that type of thinking keeps you remaining a victim. When people come to terms with accepting reality, they receive the boldness to press for healed relationships. I suggest you do some reading on the vast material, addressing traits of a healthy family system."*

Therapists often have difficulty working with the passive-aggressive person because of missing coping skills. Passive-aggressors usually sabotage the work of personal transformation. In order to unravel the chaos, it is necessary to first view behavioral patterns from a retrospective process. When you recognize a hit by passive-aggressive people, if you journal the reality of coming face to face with the truth and then take healthy action steps, you will be effective in untangling the relationship. The paramount challenge is getting the passive-aggressive person to take responsibility for their own choices.

As a counselor and life-coach, I know a person cannot heal what they refuse to acknowledge. People are also unable to heal if they are unwilling to be accountable for their own actions. Furthermore, if a person shifts blame and does not see that some of the relational problems come from within, it is impossible to bring about healing for that person. To them, their inner turmoil is a direct outcome of something which happens outside of themselves. In their minds it is others who bring them grief.

If you live with a passive-aggressive person, you may have concentrated solely on the goal to bring resolution, yet, resolution of actual issues rarely happens. If this pattern persists you will begin to feel resentment rise up within your heart. You attempt to push the resentment, hurt and pain way down inside you. The truth is, however, carrying the pain of both people leaves a person feeling emotionally ill. When resentment is unchecked it can turn to bitterness and become a stronghold in your life. If the passive-aggressor is a Christian, you feel all the more shamed to say anything negative because you don't want to appear to be judging them. Part of the reason is due to codependent thinking.

Briefly, codependency is a bent to act in overly passive or in very caretaking ways that unconstructively impacts a person's relationships and well-being. It often involves putting your own needs at a lower priority than others. One of the harmful outcomes of codependent thinking, is it may prevent people from growing or experiences consequences of their actions. Codependency does not refer to all caring behavior or feelings, but only those that are imbalanced to an unhealthy degree. If you are dealing with codependent tendencies, you will need to learn the balance of healthy assertiveness and healthy caring. I encourage you to do further reading on the subject of codependency.

*Power Tool: *"Ladies, take a moment to write down what you have learned so far. After journaling, this may be a great place to pause before going on to the next section."*

~ *Prayer* ~

"El Shaddai, who is the God Almighty, who is full of grace; I thank you for letting me see any unhealthy trends in my life and identify where I need to grow and heal. I pray for divine wisdom. I choose to walk towards the road of restoration."

~ VICTORY TOOLS ~

"Those, who trust in the Lord, will find new strength. They will soar high on the wings of eagles. They will run and not grow weary. They will walk and not faint." (Isaiah 40:31)

Chapter 8

The Subtle Seduction ~
Passive-aggressive Relationships

"What shall we say about such wonderful things as these? If God is for us, who can ever be against us?" (Romans 8:31)

During one of my conference retreats, several women shared how good it was to hear the testimonies of others. They expressed their relief at hearing they were not alone in their confusion or challenge. The stories seemed to put some clarity to understanding how passive-aggressive invalidation plays out in a person's life. Dear sisters, the spiral effect of being connected to a passive-aggressive person is very subtle. *I have found that uncovering the seductive traits of passive aggression does not come to a person's awareness until they have entered into a chaotic cycle.* As the woman does her own healing and obtains tools, the power of passive aggression changes. Not only will the women's response change but so will the thinking patterns. When the P-A person's behavior loses its affect, the patterns will break. Why? The reason is because you step out of the passive-aggressive dance.

The following descriptive scenario of one woman's path to freedom will hopefully unlock just how subtly a person can become ensnared. Also, it is meant to demonstrate how the patterns and behaviors slowly creep up on a person. As you read through this example of a married women, see what you can relate with and then do your own connecting of the dots. You may not be married, but this might provide a template to write your own story.

Family System Impact and Pre-marriage: The woman was the oldest in a family of five children. The home was safe. Everyone was permitted to develop their own unique identity. There was laughter and adventure. There was no abuse in the family of origin. Both parents were professional, and educated. The child was taught to be a responsible person. In fact, being a responsible person was a core value. Each person was given permission to choose if they wanted to go to college, however, it was an unspoken rule that they would attend. The dad, who was loving, was away a lot due to his job. The mother was encouraging and was very involved in her church. The family took vacations and parents were involved in children's activities. The mother was more involved than dad.

Missing pieces in the Family: Emotional support was missing in the family from both parents. The dad lacked emotional connection to the family. This occurred due to his job and his emotionally shut down family of origin. The mother was task-oriented and not emotionally or relationally connected to the children. The oldest child was very close to her dad. This oldest daughter did not receive emotional support. No one talked about emotions such as fears, anger, sadness, disappointments or sorrow. There was definitely disapproval if tears were shed. So the unspoken rule was, "Tears are unacceptable." This rule planted a seed, that the children would not receive comfort, so you had better learn to take care of yourself. When the daughter was eight-years-old the mother had to go back to work. The consistent encouragement and support of the mother was now sporadic, since the mother would frequently be tired from working all day. This oldest daughter became a surrogate parent to her siblings.

Seeds giving birth to Distorted Belief System: Over time, the belief system which sprouted was that emotional support will not happen in this family. The message became that emotions were bad, so don't express or acknowledge them to anyone, not even yourself.

The pattern of not expressing and not asking for help released another cycle. First, suppressing emotions was imperative for emotional survival. This led to a path where emotions went underground. This submersion of emotions is known as frozen emotions. Secondly, you feel alone with emotional struggles, because it is not acceptable to voice them to others. Conflict of any sort, later became "bad" and so the person was taught to not speak how they truly felt. These self-reliance and performance-oriented behaviors were valued and praised in various circles at school, as well as, in the faith-based communities.

Spouses Family Background: The husband came from a home where his father was critical and verbally negative. Mother was an enabling, controlling codependent. Parents did not value or attend the son's sports events. There were no responsibilities given in and around the home, and thus, he did not experience consequences. The family dealt with many prejudices and practiced traditional legalism. The outgrowth of this environment left the person feeling inadequate, insecure, fearful, lost and filled with shame messages. This person's family role was as a rebel and family stress reliever. Therefore, he learned to put on a chameleon mask, by becoming whatever a person wanted him to be to receive validation. Frequently, he connected himself with perceived powerful people in order to be in their presence and appear the same way in the eyes of others. Passive-aggressive behaviors are hidden from him, yet, he has started showing the behaviors.

Marriages: The woman was attracted to the man because of his fun, likable personality and similar profession. He was attracted to the woman because she was confident, motivated, and responsible. However, his inner turmoil was that he felt threatened, and inadequate. Over a period of time, this inner turmoil led him to begin to label his wife as his enemy.

The Discovery: The woman learned she had married a person with passive-aggressive traits. The first five years of the marriage went smoothly. Things changed after the children were born. Fears, inadequacies and feelings of being overwhelmed emerged as the man had increased responsibilities. Children took away from the man's time. He wanted a carefree existence and the woman wanted, and valued, a person who was responsible. Trust became faltering, but her childhood rule of not showing emotions kicked-in. Thus, the woman began to protect the children by taking over the leadership to make sure things were taken care of for the family. This reinforced his acting like a "little boy" but he also resented the woman being the leader. In some situations, the woman was also being more responsible.

Covert- Aggression in Full Flow: After twenty years of a slow and subtle seductive process, a passive-aggressive relationship was in place. Most of the time the marriage was functional, however about 35 percent of the time, the woman walked across a minefield. Everything was calm before the storm ensued, as soon as the man walked in the door. As soon as he arrived, he started with accusations. *"Why did you put my food in a plate on the stove?"* You answer, *"I put the food on a plate, because that is how you said you wanted it if you were going to be late."* Right away confusion is on the scene. The rules changed to throw you off balance, which is consistent with passive aggression. He finds something else to make a comment about which brings an unsettled feeling. Nothing is ever good enough from the members of the family. *"Why did you fold the clothes like that, you know I hate that? How come the kids are making so much noise? Why do we have to go to the meeting tonight?"* This barrage of questions and complaints would persist until he was emptied out. Then, he would be so nice to everyone and start making jokes. This subtle seductive cycle is crazy-making and creates frustration and confusion. Ladies, can you relate to any of these above signs?

~ PASSIVE-AGGRESSIVE EMOTIONAL CHAOS UNLEASHED ~

As the progression continues, signs of passive aggression emerge and chaos is unleashed in the relationship. The following is a sampling of the voices of women who are, or have been, connected with a passive-aggressive person. The information below is from the observations of women who have shared the subtly seductive ways passive-aggressive chaos infiltrated their relationships over a period of time.

Intimidation:
- Overt and covert behaviors such as loud and harsh tones of voice.
- Frustrated and angry facial expressions.
- Body stance became threatening.
- Impatience and quick agitation, if things did not go their way.
- Angrily phases things such as: *"Stop doing that; get out of the way; shut–up, sit down and be quiet; get in the car now."*
- Behavior instills fear, powerlessness, and that something I am doing is bad.

Explosion:
- Raging cycles and then they would be done. They act like everything is fine and go into a nice, sweet pattern.
- The cycle leaves a person wounded and confused. Inside him he feels, stupid and feels like he cannot do anything right.

Actions:
- Slamming doors, yanking things, or raising fists in a threatening fashion.
- Immature tantrums.
- If asked to make a decision, the person would answer in an irritated tone.
- If asked to assist with a project, the person would procrastinate or become frustrated.
- Over time, the woman makes an internal vow that she cannot need the person for anything. The woman finally says, "Okay, I am on my own and I must be self-sufficient."

Worn and Torn Down:
- The behavior is not cherishing, nurturing, comforting or protecting.

- The behavior is tearing and wearing you down, undermining, de-valuing and destroying your self-esteem.
- The treatment is not the Lord's plan and only you can stop the cycle. You must start setting healthy boundaries.

Internal Feelings:
- Hurt because the man didn't care enough about the family to make a change or seek help.
- Alone and isolated and had to be silent about the reality of passive aggression.
- Felt betrayed, devalued, ashamed and angry.
- Guilty as a Christian woman who had been taught to honor and respect her spouse.

Women Respond to the Chaotic Behavior:
- Fix-it by rescuing.
- Denial by convincing self, the situation is not so bad.
- Keep it all hidden, especially to other believers.
- Try to reason with the person, however, the man's filter would rise up creating sulking, or fear of failure.
- Women take on guilt that it is their fault with statements like, "*I made him feel bad*, so what can I do to fix this situation?"
- No resolution, so no way to move forward.

The Christian Beliefs which Enable a Cover-Up:
- The Lord is pleased with my sacrificial choices.
- Obedience means blessings, regardless of unhealthy patterns.
- Mean and difficult people are won by a gentle and quiet spirit through respect, loyalty and honor. At times, this belief might be backed up by using scripture incorrectly.
- Other people come first. Your needs for love, significance, safety and security are not as important as other people's needs.
- Taking care of self is being self-centered and selfish.
- Distorted faith-based belief systems form bondages and will hold a person captive if not re-aligned with the truth of the Word.

Power Tool: *"Women will need to break free of unhealthy beliefs in order to start the healing process. Remember, the statements below and they will help as you break free of the chaotic cyclic behaviors of passive-aggressive relationships."*

- Identify and replace the lies which took root and keep you in the dark. Replace the lies with the truth. Jesus promises us truth is what sets us free. Read John 8:32 and memorize this verse for strength in times of confusion.
- Grieve and then reframe a healthy lifestyle.
- Declare that in your brokenness, The Lord can move to heal your heart while receiving His grace, comfort, compassion, protection, boldness, clarity and forgiveness.
- Made a decision to step out in faith and not by sight.
- Seek help with safe supportive community groups as you learn to set clear and healthy boundaries. There may be a time when you need to receive counseling. Ladies, do not hesitate if you need to seek counseling in developing the skills of integrating boundaries to break codependency, enabling and rescuing traits. Learning to set boundaries, apart from being emotional, will require stating facts and learning to ask for what you need without being controlling.
- Accept yourself entirely with the good, bad and ugly. Regain your God-given identity.
- Understand one of the keys to freedom is taking personal ownership for your thoughts and actions.
- Learn to say no to harmful behaviors. It is okay to protect yourself from any form of abuse.
- Determine to no longer tolerate put-downs or shaming patterns from others.
- Purpose to be intentional in taking back your voice. You are worthy! Ladies, you might have to practice standing in front of a mirror and say, "I am worthy!

My sisters, take time to do the work of healing and do not run to a quick fix. A restorative process will not have lasting results until the healing steps become an integral part of your life. Keep putting into practice all you have learned and remember it is a process which cannot be forced. The Lord will be your joy and strength.

*Power Tool: *"You have done a lot of process work, so I want to stress how important it is to have a bit of fun. Laughter and fun are medicine for the soul. Yes, I really know, some of you are very busy, but take time to smell the roses!* Resting and refreshing is part of healing and restoration."

~ *Prayer* ~

"Abba Father, I pray you allow me to see and healthily deal with the emotional triggers throughout my daily life. Help me respond in a new way with freedom, grace and gentleness. Thank you that I am unshackled and able to face my future. I ask you to order my steps. Amen."

Chapter 9

Breaking the Cycles ~
Impacting Generational Change

"There is no one like the Lord. He rides across the heavens to help you, across the skies in majestic splendor. The eternal Lord is your refuge, and His everlasting arms are under you . . . (Deuteronomy 33:26- 27)

Your health and positive relational change are important. However, equally foundational in writing this book is providing enough information and practical tools to also bring about generational change. I honor you, daughters of the King, because you have chosen the path of serenity. You have faced challenges and painful realities in order to experience peaceful, emotional, relational and spiritual health. There are specific steps you can add to the toolkit you've accumulated from previous chapters. These tools will assist you in fulfilling and receiving healing today and hope for tomorrow. Each step will sow seeds of new choices and reap new beginnings.

My sisters, breaking destructive cycles will be one of the most difficult journeys you will ever do. However, the journey will bring freedom. At some point you must confront and make a decision that what you are living under is not what you want to pass on to the next generation. It is my desire and prayer that as healing comes, sons, daughters, grandsons and granddaughters will not carry the learned patterns of passive-aggressive behaviors into their future relationships. As you read this chapter, please stay alert to the leading of the Holy Spirit. I encourage you to journal what you are learning as it is revealed to you throughout this healing process.

Your strength to walk in victory will come pouring from heaven as you utilize the knowledge of the passive-aggressive tactics and then choose to break the cycles. Proverbs 3:5 gives us a promise. It says, *"Trust in the Lord with all your heart; do not depend on your own understanding. Seek His will in all you do, and He will show you which path to take."* Now, your next faith step is to claim the promise that the Lord will direct your path. The more you take action and apply the steps to freedom, the less power the passive-aggressive behaviors will have in controlling your actions, thereby, freeing you from being continually victimized. When it feels like you cannot go one more step, the Lord will pick you up. The footprint in the sand will be Him carrying you and giving you rest by abiding in His loving arms.

"Joyful are those who have the God as their helper . . . whose hope is in the Lord their God. He made heaven and earth, the sea, and everything in them. He keeps every promise forever." (Psalm 146:5-6)"

SO YOU WANT A BREAKTHROUGH ~ STEP OUT of DENIAL

In general, denial is usually a coping mechanism that permits a person some time to get it together. This time is about adjusting to a distressing situation and distressful emotional conflict. It allows a person to sit for a minute in light of painful thoughts, threatening information, and anxiety by refusing to acknowledge facts that are obvious to others. However, when denial stays too long, it will interfere with a person's full healing process and ultimately prolong the journey of pain. The fact is you will be as sick as your secrets. Putting truth into the light prevents the Enemy from using darkness to keep people in bondage. Denial can be blinding and harmful relationally, while keeping you in a state of rationalization, oppression, suppression and depression. Denial, in one way or another is a protective mechanism which involves four components:

1. Denial refuses to acknowledge certain situations.
2. Denial avoids the fact and realities of the situation.
3. Denial minimizes the consequences of the situation.
4. Denial attempts to fix, rationalizes unhealthy behaviors and rescue others.

The main action step in breaking generational cycles is to come out of denial. Truth is the antidote to denial. We must recognize root issues of the past and acknowledge them in light of truth. However, it is equally valuable to focus on current options and take the responsibility to come out of denial. The following acronym breaks down the results of **D.E.N.I.A.L.**:

- **D ~ depressing**, painful memories and emotions prolong resolution and healing. If unresolved, wounds and emotions will be buried alive. As we've referred to previously, the outcome of this protective mechanism is called *frozen emotions*.
  2 Peter 2:19 promises freedom as you unwrap the roots of the frozen emotions.

- **E ~ expressing** false emotions by pretending everything is fine. This results in unexplained and unresolved issues. **Psalm 139:23-24** tells us the Holy Spirit will search the heart and pinpoint the truth, which sets us free.

- **N ~ numbness**, which immobilizes potential growth. Feeling numb may prevent healing because walls are put up during periods of wounding. When you read **Psalm 107:13** you understand that as we cry out to the Lord, He is near to us and will remove any shameful or painful messages.

- **I ~ Internal turmoil** creates anxiety, detachment and depression, which can separate you from self and others. **1 John 1:4-7** reinforces the truth that God is the light in the midst of darkness. When truth is exposed, feelings of powerlessness and anxiety are decreased.

- **A ~ avoiding** confrontation of reality means unmet needs will foster emotional distance and then sabotage relationships. Staying in denial allows a person to continue justifying, minimizing, fixing and rescuing others instead of focusing on personal recovery. **Philippians 1:6** promises that if you step out of denial and face the truth in your life, you can be certain that the Lord, who began a good work within you, will continue His work until it is finished.

- **L ~ living in denial** only prolongs the seasons of pain and grief. My sisters, claim the word in **Jeremiah 30:17** which says, "*I will give you back your health and heal your wounds, says the Lord . . .*"

After looking at the outcomes of remaining in denial, it's obvious the healthy option is to step out of denial and crack the combination. The only code you need to confront denial is truth. So many times we hear the words, "to know the truth and the truth will set us free." Yet, I know many people who know the truth but do not live free lives. Sisters, we must know, act, speak and live out the precepts of truth. We must be ready to ask ourselves is this truth in my life? If not, why? *You have to practice living out the truth. The Holy Spirit will direct your steps in moving from the head knowledge of truth, to walking it out daily.* When you practice living in truth it is more than head knowledge, it becomes heart wisdom. The next step is finding a way to keep a healthy balance. While denial does have a place in the early stages of grief and recovery, here are a few strategies to begin moving beyond denial.

1. Recognize there is a time to chill and reflect, as well as, a season to take action. Allow yourself some grace. During the

chill-and-reflect times, it is okay to give yourself permission to say, "I just can't think about all the drama right now." However, if you find yourself repeatedly saying this for extended periods of time, recognize the red flag and ask yourself if it's time to move ahead in the healing process. If so, Dear Ones, it is time to pray, journal, and reach out to a safe person. In doing so, it will help prevent you from getting into a rut or struck in place of immobilization. The Enemy thrives when Christian's become immobilized and dwell on hurtful actions.

2. Be honest with yourself. Ask if there are still any fears preventing you from processing and bringing resolution to your situation. You may require help getting to the root of the fear. Do not hesitate to reach out and seek the help you need.

3. Write down potential negative consequences if you don't take any action steps.

4. Try to identify and get to the root of any irrational beliefs you have about the situation. It is important to understand and name the emotional triggers in unhealthy relationships.

UNCOVER and HEAL ~ ROOTS of EMOTIONAL TRIGGERS

Ladies, take a moment to write down what you have learned so far. After journaling, this may be a great place to pause before going on to the next section.

> *"Let us test and examine our ways, and let us turn back to the Lord."(Lamentations 3:40)*

Ladies, after you step out of denial and acknowledge you have a relational challenge. You will face the unpredictable behavior of a passive-aggressive person, and be triggered. Do you remember being on the playground in grade school and getting on the seasaw? You go up and down. The other kid waits until you are having fun, and up in the air. Then all of a sudden, they jump off. Yes, you know what happens next! Bam!! You hit the ground and as you turn, you see the kid running away and laughing. The passive-aggressive person gains your trust; get you on an emotional seasaw and jumps off. You may not have time to stop and access what just happened, however, you are bewildered. One tool I call, *"Hot Pen Writing"* can be used to off-load the immediate frustration or other emotions. Writing can be random and one word or one sentence phrases. When using this tool, you write some quick thoughts which you can expand on at a later time, if necessary.

***Power Tool**: *"This quick tool will help prevent you from shutting down. It will also bring clarity and understanding to your situation. Take time to journal your expanded thoughts from the hot pen writing and read it out loud. What are you thinking right now?"*

If you are still having a hard time getting to the roots of an issue, you may need to progress to the next level and utilize another tool. The **S.T.O.P.** tool is useful in laying groundwork for that discovery. Unhealed wounds must be identified in order for you to experience release and restoration. Any unhealed areas become fair game for the Enemy to use to continue to generate disunity, shame, fear or an inability to set boundaries. The following tool can assist you in exposing the roots and any internal turmoil involved. It is the Lord's desire that you deal with the root. Has the Holy Spirit been tugging at your heart, trying to let you know it is time to step towards healing?

The **S.T.O.P.** tool is a way to start discovering the emotional impact of dealing with the web and world of passive-aggressive cycles. So many times women have stated it is hard to identify what is happening. They cannot pinpoint the roots of their hurts, needs or feelings. This tool can also assist in identifying triggers which lead to certain behaviors, emotions or ways of thinking patterns. The **S.T.O.P.** tool is only one way of identifying core roots. Learning to pay attention to inner signals and then practicing appropriate ways to meet needs and resolve issues will enhance your serenity and healing journey:

- **S ~ Seek the truth.** When we feel wounded, we may need to discern the truth covering an *internal hunger*. If we are hungry physically, we can become more easily irritated and frustrated. However, if you are hungry for affection, affirmation, significance, love or security, there is a void in the heart. Also, there will be a tendency to avoid setting boundaries. Fear and doubt can surface if we believe others will reject or abandon us if we set healthy boundaries. Another consideration is to look at how you are filling this void. Is it shopping, eating, or being connected to unhealthy or toxic people? Maybe it is an avoidance pattern or an emotional detachment mechanism you have set in motion. *How are you protecting yourself from being hurt?*

- **T ~ Take the time.** We must take time to determine if there is anger in your heart. When you have been struggling with the ongoing frustration from passive-aggressive cycles, it is not uncommon to deal with anger, resentment and bitterness. Anger is not a primary emotion. It is a warning flag which will tell you there is something going on in your heart and mind. You must ask yourself what is going on underneath the anger. Are you feeling insecure, hurt, fearful, minimized, invalidated or vulnerable? *What negative thoughts are you replaying in your mind?*

- **O ~ Open up.** Feeling wounded can shut our emotions down, which can cause internal loneliness. *Loneliness* is very different than being *alone*. People choose to be alone. However, loneliness comes from deep inside and you may feel no one understands the depth of your hurt. Some women have felt, "*I just have to work this out alone. This is my secret. I can't tell anyone.*" You can be in a crowd of a thousand people and still feel lonely, isolated and empty internally. Loneliness creates a sense of being detached, confused or disconnected. The worst thing you can do is to isolate yourself when feeling lonely and abandoned. You must open up to the healing the Holy Spirit has for you. You can connect with other safe people. Remember, safe people; tell you the truth with love, grace, and compassion. *Who are the emotionally safe and supportive people in your life?*

- **P ~ Press-in and focus on healing.** Women frequently multitask and can physically burnout by wearing too many hats. Fatigue lowers a person's defenses and can leave you vulnerable physically, emotionally and spiritually. Being tired can disrupt your daily functioning patterns. You must press-in and focus on your own healing process. Ladies, make sure you get rest when you are tired physically and emotionally. In dealing with passive-aggressive people, it is not uncommon to become tired of _____ *(fill in the blank).* For example, you may be tired of things not changing. It is time to take action to stop the cycle. *What voice do you need? What are you tolerating? What are you putting off in confronting or setting a boundary?*

You do not need to experience all of these components, in order to stop, listen and look at what is truly triggering you. However, if you are dealing with any one of the above areas, then you need to explore the root of the reason. For example, if you are triggered by someone's comment and anger starts to rise up inside, you might ask, *"What am I really feeling? Am I feeling criticized? Am I being treated like a child?"* Then, you must say, I have to **S.T.O.P.,** and see what is going on inside. You may only need to pray or simply journal to gain perspective. Other times, it is important to speak specifically to the person. For instance, if you are feeling minimized, you might communicate to the person with direct statements. **Here are some beginning guidelines for your healthy direct communication:**

- Use statements that explain your feeling rather than thought. Stating: **"I feel …"** is much clearer than saying, **"I think …"**
- Use specific statements about what action you observed. "When … happens."
- State what you would like to see happen. "I would like …"
- Use statements that take ownership of your role in the challenge. "I will …"

- By the end of the conversation have some sort of follow through to the statements. You should seek an actual resolution of action. Otherwise, you will not have accomplished much with the communication. For example: "So, what we are saying is you will do ... and I will do ..."

Let's look at an example of how clear communication can be a useful tool:

- "I feel devalued when I am talking with you about our son's school work and you continue to read the paper.
- When that happens, I do not feel as though I am being heard.
- I would like you to stop reading the paper when I am sharing with you.
- I will be sure to communicate that I would like your attention to discuss a specific topic.
- Will you do that?

* **Power Tool:** *Ladies, it is vital you identify personal triggers in developing a proactive plan with passive-aggressive people. The information you have gained to this point should have given you an idea of your own triggers. Grab your journal and make a list of the triggers you are able to name and then see if you can identify the root cause of them.*

~ PERSONAL TRIGGERS and FROZEN EMOTIONS ~

At other times, certain emotions become frozen and become shut down whenever the adult feels a **R.A.T.** (Means: **R**ealizes hurt, **A**ttack/**A**bandonment /**T**urmoil), which is an acronym to assist in identifying buried emotions and memories. This is a tool which can be used by the passive-aggressive person, as well as, the person being impacted. **Passive aggression is frequently a reaction to feeling rejected, attacked, abandoned or inner turmoil**. These feelings can be real or perceived. Part of healing is learning to get to the root of issues. It is important to listen to self-talk and replace any lies or distortions with healthy thinking and beliefs. Self-talk are negative thoughts you tell yourself, which can become destructive. Such as, "I never do anything right? I am so stupid." Exposing the reason behind the emotions leads to getting to the real you and removing the protective mask.

R ~ Realize the hurt of rejection. Often this stems from lack of parental blessings, lack of affirmations, sibling comparisons, or general criticism. Acknowledging the roots allows you institute proactive tools.

A ~ Attacks or feelings of abandonment create lasting pain that goes deep. If a person experiences spiritual, physical, emotional or verbal wounds from significant people in their life, they retain a sense of abandonment into their current relationships.

T ~ Turmoil has created feelings of inadequacy, insignificance and inferiority that threaten a person's identity and self-talk. The inner turmoil feels emotionally threatening and a survival skill will kick in to prevent further feeling so powerlessness or hurt. A few examples of protective behaviors are: 1) defensiveness, 2) sarcastic remarks, 3) dismissing language.

*Power Tool: *"It's important to note, when you start using any healthy tool with a person who is passive aggressive, they have a tendency to try and stop you. The attempt will be made immediately after your first statement to them addresses a specific situation. You may say, "I feel such and such." The passive-aggressive person may immediately tell you, "you are wrong in how you feel."*

Dear ones, do not become defensive, simply repeat your statements. Otherwise, if you begin to defend your feeling statement, the passive-aggressive person will try to detour you by saying something similar to the following response: *"I have feelings too and so I am just sharing my feeling."* Often, when dealing with a passive-aggressive person you attempt to have each other share feelings and thoughts in order to bring resolution. However, the passive-aggressive will attempt to detour you and flip the script.

Triggers caused by R.A.T. experiences are potentially inroads for the Enemy. He will employ tactics to rob, steal and destroy a person's inner peace, hope and freedom, if any R.A.T. events remain unhealed." The Holy Spirit will reveal the enemy's working in your life by showing you truth, which opens spiritual eyes. You will receive red flag moments to process and journal. As you journal, it will begin to identify the patterns you are dealing with on a regular basis. Sisters, the red flags are warning signs which are designed to attract your attention. Stay Alert!

~ *Prayer* ~

"Lord, thank you for guiding me around the snares and roadblocks of the enemy. I choose to declare that victory is mine! I pray for courage to gain more understanding of how to stand boldly and win the battles."

Chapter 10

Getting To the Real Deal ~
Lifting the Confusion

"Take delight in the Lord, and He will give you the desires of your heart." (Psalm37:4)

Ladies, if you are dealing with a passive-aggressor, at times, in order to keep your mind focused in the event of a potential detour tactic, you must be aware of what you are feeling, thinking and believing, while being proactive. One of the ways to identify your own triggers and response patterns is to journal, so you can develop a proactive plan for the future. **"Getting Real"** is one of those journaling tools. After you have completed enough of these written exercises, when an event threatens to throw you off track, you will have a proactive tool already in place. You are then positively empowered.

I encourage you to keep telling yourself the truth as you continue your journey. In connecting with many women, I have seen the confusion lifted from practicing the tool of journaling. One of the benefits is you see in black and white what you are already experiencing. Journaling gives you retrospective knowledge in the early stage of breaking the silence. Denial is a hallmark tendency in a passive-aggressive relationship. Invite the Holy Spirit into your healing process as you use the *"Getting Real"* tool. **The Holy Spirit**

will reveal areas you are excusing, rationalizing, avoiding or minimizing. I encourage you to journal your thoughts, in order to uncover truth and live in reality.

The next time you are impacted by a Dr. Jekyll and Mr. Hyde passive-aggressive experience, record your observations using the following format. Find a quiet spot and sit down with your journal. Before you start to write, take time and pray for the Holy Spirit to reveal any personal blind spots. Allow the reality to come forth. The Holy Spirit will be faithful to give clarity, and truth will surface as you go through the following process of the *"Getting Real"* tool. It will assist you in knowing what steps are needed in the future to develop healthy life skills, which will enhance healthy living. The truth, even though it may hurt, will permit you to walk in an enlightened, victorious mindset. This tool will also unveil the way you enter into a passive-aggressive dance. When you understand how you might get hooked, then you can take action steps in order to break out of personally destructive cycles.

GETTING TO THE REAL DEAL ~ JOURNAL PROCESS

1. Describe the situational facts which brought up various negative triggers.
2. List the feelings and emotions you are currently experiencing, as close to the event as possible. Some of the emotions may include feeling threatened, angry, lonely, afraid, powerless, exposed, vulnerable, diminished and devalued.
3. Ponder this question based on the list of feelings in Step 2: When I feel this way, what do I believe about myself and the other person? For example, you may believe if you say any-thing, things will only get worse.
4. Next, recognize repetitive negative self-talk. What are you telling yourself about the situation? What actions have been taken based on your negative self-talk?
5. Describe your normal plan of action. What actions do I nor-mally take? For example; do you try harder to please, withdraw, rescue, or attempt to fix the situation?

6. Describe how this response harms me? *(Self-esteem may take a nose-dive)*
7. How does this response or action harm others? *(It may be that your response isolates them.)*
8. What do I get from actions I take? *What is the payoff?* Does it minimize further pain?
9. What is the truth of this immediate situation? *Are you fearful?* If so, of what or who?
10. Ask yourself, if you have any unmet needs? If so, what are they? *(Validation, honesty, follow-through, affirmation or affection.)*
11. Describe how you will replace your old behavior the next time the trigger surfaces. What's your proactive strategy for responding to similar situations in the future?
12. Be honest about how you feel. Instead of saying, *"I am concerned about ..."* try owning the reality by stating, *"I am scared."* Learning to be honest with yourselves, paves the way to be honest with others. Passive-aggressive people have a great deal of difficulty expressing their honest feeling. So, when you step out of the dance and speak truthfully and honestly, you model healthy communication.
13. Ask yourself if you are responding to a false belief communicated by the passive-aggressive person. If so, replace it with the truth. For example, if they say, *"All you want to do is start arguments"* and they walk away and leave you standing hurt. Ask, is this true? What part may be true? If false, do not activate a self-talk pattern which leads you down a distorted path. Say out loud, *"I was not starting an argument. I was simply asking for clarification."* Otherwise, you might begin self talk similar to, *"Why do I feel so guilty, when I haven't done anything wrong."*
14. Ask the Lord to give you the courage, boldness and strength to be consistent and committed. I have had some of my clients write a letter to the Lord and then wait for a response from Him. Write the response from the Lord and read it out loud. Some have said, *"I tried it and I did not hear from the Lord."* I always remind them to, keep practicing the exercise. Just as He has for them, He will give you something to write, in His timing. It may be you need to use that time to be quiet and rest in the Lord. It

is important to be accountable, while setting healthy boundaries and making restorative changes.

STAYING FOCUSED ~ KEEPING YOUR BOUNDARIES

Another communication tool used in clarifying emotions and practicing a safe process to resolve situations is one that brings continued focus. Frequently, when there have been continual unresolved issues in relationships, there may not be a safe way to get to the roots. If the relationship with the passive-aggressive person has seemed to go round-and-round and the same subjects and other issues get pulled in, you'll need to use this tool. Similar to the *"Getting to the Real Deal Tool,"* the *"Staying Focused"* tool has several parts leading to a potential resolution. Each part has specific questions to communicate to others in an attempt to seek clarity, and bring resolution in a non-threatening way. Obtaining resolution is very difficult to achieve when communicating with passive aggressive people. These unresolved issues remain open wounds, which continually trigger hurt and fertile ground for passive aggression. These questions can be used after you have discovered the triggers in specific relationships or circumstances.

Part 1 ~ Express and describe actual facts. The outcome will be to identify and address the realities of a given situation.
- "I have seen or heard..." You are describing facts only. What you have seen and heard.
- "I presume ..." You share your thoughts identifying what you think is going on.
- "I am curious if..." You give a positive statement to include the facts and your feelings.
- "My impression is that ..." You share what you suppose about the other person. You address what you believe are the reasons certain behaviors continue to crop up.
- "I think if..." Share your perspective of the effect on the relationship, if certain behaviors continue.

Part 2 ~ Express specifically how you feel. The outcome is to share your emotions, without becoming emotional, by staying focused on specific emotional triggers. If you are too emotional it might stop or interfere with speaking clearly, directly, honestly and succinctly.

- "I am confused by..." State what is creating your confusion. Incorporate the pattern when appropriate.
- "I dislike ..." State how you are feeling, in a clear fashion.
- "I am upset and discouraged by..." Be specific with an example or two.
- "I feel sorry that ..." Take ownership for the reason you have not confronted, talked about or dealt with the challenge in the past. For example, give the reason you haven't set healthy boundaries in the past.
- "I am fearful of..." This statement is usually based on the previous experiences in the relationship. You may want to give specific examples for clarification or to emphasize a point.
- "I am irritated by..." Address a behavioral pattern, or cycle, and the repeated outcome if nothing has changed or been resolved.

Part 3 ~ Express a potential path for resolution. The outcome of this path is to not stay in the replaying of the emotions and hurt.

- "I am contented when..." You need to describe what you want for yourself, others and for the relationship. Cast a vision for change.
- "I would like ..." You must be very specific about your requests, even if you have tried the suggestion in the past.

Part 4 ~ Express positive forward action. The outcome leads you toward action steps by stating specific and appropriate boundaries. This path allows you to walk past your fears.

- "I anticipate ..." Talk about what you will do to improve the situation. Remember to use, "I" statements, while looking at the future, the past actions and the current situation.
- "I value ..." Share affirmation for the person or the healthy actions being made to bring resolution. Communicate your expectations and include what is no longer tolerable or acceptable to you.

Part 5 ~ Express the realities of what it will take to change a behavior or belief. The outcome stops you from minimizing and rationalizing the truth of the cycles.

- "I recognize it will…" Be vigorously honest with yourself and verbalize what you are aware of and what it will take to be healed. The "I recognize" step is designed to address the reality not the potential. I understand it will take some time for "_____" to occur.

Part 6 ~ Express a desire for a solution. The outcome is to cast a vision for the future.

- "I look forward to or I am hopeful that…" Do not communicate false hopes, but be positive where you can, in order to move forward.

Part 7 ~ Express an action plan. The outcome in using this component is getting a commitment and having accountability in place to stay focused and consistent. This path also prevents sabotaging cycles.

- "Will you do…?" If you make a request which is very important to you. Check and make sure you are on the same page, so boundaries and expectations are clear. If you need to move to a problem solving process, schedule to do so at another time. For example, *"I would like for us to discuss this again on Saturday, so we have an agreement on what we are to do to have date nights out. Will that work for you? If not tell me what will work."* Stop putting off addressing issues. It only creates more of a divide in the relationship. If the issue you are addressing has been a long term unresolved issue, it is time to set a healthy boundary. Now, my sisters, if the passive-aggressive person begins to make excuses or does not give you a concrete answer, then the following is the next step to take:
- Restate your request and then add the action step you will take. For example: *"I would like you to call me if you are not going to be home for dinner by 5:00pm. However, if I do not hear from you by then, the children and I will go ahead and eat."*

~ PRACTICING THE STAYING FOCUSED TOOL ~

The following is an example of using all the components of the *"Staying Focused"* tool. Again, this is a communication tool which may be used when addressing a specific, difficult issue and unresolved cyclic behaviors.

- I have seen that when you come home in the evening, you go straight to the garage and do not say hello to me, or the children.
- I presume you want to spend time with us, even though it may not appear to be your desire.
- I am curious if you come home and avoid us because you are exhausted from the work day.
- My impression is that you would prefer to separate yourself instead of connecting with your family.
- I think if you choose to isolate every night, it affects our family.
- I'm confused by the irritation in your voice, when I relayed the boys and I feel devalued. I'm at a complete loss by the fact that you stated an effort would be made to connect with the boys when you come home from work, yet that has not occurred for several weeks.
- I dislike when I bring this pattern to your attention you get irritated and upset. Yet, you keep making promises to spend quality time with the boys. I feel the promises made are empty since there is no follow through after our discussions.
- I'm upset and discouraged by watching the boys try to talk with you and your response remains, "I'll listen after I finish reading the paper." However, that time rarely comes and they become very disappointed.
- I feel sorry for not addressing this issue sooner. I am also exhausted over trying to fix it and making excuses as to why their dad has not made time for some interaction each day. I realize it is necessary for me to stop fixing, rescuing and making excuses.
- I'm fearful, that this is an old pattern of behavior rearing its head again.

- I'm irritated by the constant tension in our relationships. It seems the most we do is to disappear into separate areas of the house. I am exasperated by this disconnect in our family.
- I'm contented when we can spend some family time together each evening.
- I would like us to communicate our feelings about issues in a less overbearing way in the future.
- I anticipate if we all make an effort to understand each other it will help us communicate in healthier ways. I think, an intentionally set aside time for problem solving, would be a start to bringing resolution.
- I value the time you spend providing for your family.
- I recognize you are tired and may need some down time before engaging with the family.
- I look forward to sitting down together and devising an action plan to resolve this problem.
- Will you set a time aside for us to talk and devise a plan? What time and day will work well for you?

You can also use this tool when you are personally triggered by an event which feels like a *"slap back."* A woman, who I walked with through the healing journey, coined this term. It means, when you are triggered, you feel the painful memories of the original past event, as though it was just occurring. You get caught off guard and have to regroup your thoughts. Have any of you had this experience, where a familiar situation happens, yet, you are at a lost for words? Then two hours later, you replay the scenario out loud, stating everything you wanted to say. Yes, you are talking to yourself!

You can use the "Staying Focused" written exercise, not only as a communication technique, but also as a personal process tool. By journaling, you are developing a proactive skill. As you look retrospectively, it will empower you to have a voice the next time a similar circumstance arises. For example, if you are triggered, you can address the roots of your feelings and view steps you will need to take to bring every thought into captivity. In the following example, see if you can name the person who is referenced.

- I have seen that when God asked us, "What we had done?" you told Him, "It was the women you gave me. She gave me the fruit from the forbidden tree."
- I presume you were afraid of what God would say, or do, to you.
- I am curious as to whether you really know how much your statement hurt me.
- My impression is you were trying to deny you had any part in what occurred.
- I think, or me, that was the worst day of my life. I felt shamed, rejected, abandoned and betrayed.
- I'm confused that you did not confess to being there when Satan showed me the fruit and you didn't say or do anything to protect me.
- I dislike you blaming me for the whole incident and now I don't feel I can trust you.
- I am discouraged because we have lived together for awhile and I thought we have an open and honest relationship.
- I feel sorry that I didn't address how I felt sooner. I regret not saying anything right after you told God it was His fault and then my fault.
- I'm fearful that if another situation comes, you will not protect me. It makes me feel insecure.
- I'm irritated that now we have this stress and tension between us.
- I would have been contented if we could have been united to confess our choice to God without blaming, when He asked us what we had done.
- I would like to trust you again, but I feel as though I don't know you anymore.
- I anticipate as we share our thoughts and start praying together, we can hopefully work on re-establishing trust.
- I value all the times we spent together in perfect harmony.
- I recognize it might take me awhile to feel safe and secure around you in the future. I also realize we have to face the consequences of our actions.
- I look forward to the time we will be able to heal our relationship. We have a lot to do together to take domain over the earth.

- Will you do that? *(There isn't a request or response needed regarding this story, because it would be your personal journaling process)*

After the first questions, I'm sure you quickly noted that this was a *Staying Focused* discussion Eve could have used with Adam in the Garden of Eden.

*****Power Tool**: *If we want to experience restoration, it is vital to commit to being honest with ourselves and others. Strength and security will come from the Lord. "I will bless the Lord who guides me; even at night my heart instructs me. I know the Lord is always with me. I will not be shaken, for he is right beside me." (Psalm 16:7-8)*

~ HEALTHY ASSERTIVE COMMUNICATION SKILLS ~

After many seminars, I read letter after letter asking the same questions. "Is there a communication toolkit of what to say when dealing with the passive-aggressive men in life?" Sisters, remember one of the goals and patterns of passive-aggressive people is to resist and sabotage perceived, or real, requests from others. The passive-aggressive person views requests by others as demands, and therefore the requests are felt as being controlling. Frustration and outbursts of hostility emerge in relationships with this belief on board. **Assertiveness is the ability to genuinely express your opinions, needs, feelings, attitudes and boundaries in a way which does not violate other's boundaries.** It is an effective approach to bring resolution to conflict. It is a way of expressing ourselves and keeping our self-worth intact, giving us the confidence to communicate without games or manipulation. It can also be applied in various interpersonal relationships such as work, family, church and significant others. Assertiveness requires being clearly forthright with integrity.

Every time, we communicate we use one of several basic forms of communication styles: assertive, aggressive, passive and passive aggressive. The healthiest style is assertive communication. Most people use a combination of styles depending on the person or situation. The communication styles we choose generally depend on what our past experiences have taught us. However, it is vital to learn communication skills to best obtain our needs, in specific situations. Practice being assertive and see how it will assist you in defusing anger, reducing guilt and strengthening personal and professional relationships.

The following information is for women in significant personal and professional relationships. The examples are designed to help you learn and practice assertiveness skills. It takes time to change, so be patient, and keep pressing forward!

- Think and talk about yourself in positive language by eliminating qualifying statements to your opinions and requests. For example, remove wording that undermines your message such as, "You'll probably think this is crazy, but. . ." or "That's just my opinion."
- Consciously take responsibility for yourself and avoid taking ownership for others by fixing, rescuing, and excusing. Eliminate "should, ought to, and have to" from your vocabulary. Instead, practice using the phrase, "I choose to…"
- Give and get information, however, say what you mean and mean what you say. Do not feel you must constantly justify your answers.
- Utilizing a polite assertive "no, thank you," to excessive requests from others, will enable you to avoid overloading your schedule and will promote balance in your life. It reduces the drama and stress in your life. For instance, instead of saying, "You're so rude! You're always late." Try saying, "We agreed to meet at 11:30 and it is now 12:30." This is sticking to the facts, which is critical when speaking to passive-aggressive people. Then describe the effects of the behavior. Do not exaggerate, judge or engage in a power struggle. Instead of, "now you have ruined our lunch time" simply state, "Now I have less time to spend for lunch with you because I still need to be back to work by 1:00."

- When addressing a passive-aggressive person, be specific. For example, "When you yell or speak in a harsh tone of voice, I feel attacked." "When you tell the kids they can do something that I've already forbidden, some of my parental authority is taken away, and I then feel undermined."
- When a passive-aggressive person in your life makes a snide remark, uses insensitive sarcasm, or hurtful humor, be calm. Firmly state you do not find that way of communicating to be acceptable and you want it to stop. Asking whether they will agree to the request, will give you a baseline to return to in the future. It also lets you determine if the person is committed to the change.
- Address all passive-aggressive behaviors as *close to the events as possible*, because the passive-aggressive person will move on and/or bury the incident. They tend to selectively forget, if situations are not brought to their attention immediately. Passive-aggressive people will strike, move on and leave you feeling stunned. *So, you must not pretend you did not experience the hit and hurt. It is real! Do not ignore these statements. Otherwise, you set up precedents for the future.* Yes, I know I am repeating this statement. The balance is confronting without permitting you to be drawn into a fuss or become detoured by excuses.
- Use repetition of a statement of fact when appropriate. For example, "I am not available at that time. Our original time is better for me."
- When your intuition and gut feelings say you are being manipulated or taken advantage of by repeated excuses, rationalizations, or apathy, you are probably correct! The key word here is *repetitious* cycles which remain unresolved. However, do not jump to conclusions until you check your perceptions with the Holy Spirit. It's essential to confirm your instincts or there may be a tendency to evaluate and act based totally on emotions. Once you have confirmed your perceptions, and stated appropriate boundaries, trust your internal instincts in the future.

*~ When wounded, remind yourself of how much
you are loved by the Lord ~*

Isaiah 41:10 says, "Do not be afraid, for I am with you. Don't be discouraged, for I am your God. I will strengthen you and help you. I will hold you up with my victorious right hand."

Philippians 4:13 says, "For *I can do everything through Christ, who gives me strength.*" Therefore, you have abilities empowered by the Lord.

Isaiah 54:10 says, "*For the mountains may move and the hills disappear, but even then my unfailing love for you will remain. My covenant of blessings will never be broken, says the Lord, who has mercy on you.*" The Lord loves us deeply and promises to be with us during the adversities of life.

Hebrews 13:6 says, "*So we can say with confidence, The Lord is my helper, so I will have no fear. What can mere people do to me?*"

~ Prayer ~

"Dear Abba Father, help me to meditate and apply your precious promises to my life. At times, I feel there are so many trails and storms. There are many circumstances to deal with in my life. Sometimes, I begin to think I am going crazy. I know you can empower me to persevere. Thank you Lord, for unveiling response patterns which may inhibit me from moving forward. I claim victory today, even while I'm in process. I choose deliverance in Jesus name. Amen"

Chapter 11

Amazing Grace of the Holy Spirit ~
In the Midst of a Broken Heart

"The Lord will be your sure foundation, providing a rich store of salvation, wisdom and knowledge . . ." (Isaiah 33:6)

Remember, the Lord is the source of strength. I have heard that over and over again. Although, completely accurate, when you are in the early stages of grief and the pain is the most difficult, it is challenging to allow this truth to sink into the heart. My sisters, I want to begin with encouragement. There is healing for your broken heart. If you have been connected with a passive-aggressive relationship, there are likely areas where your heart has broken. These areas of brokenness, disillusionment, disappointment, and inner loneliness create grief. *Walking through the grief journey is a necessary path you must do in order to be restored.* The first step involves your decision to admit you are hurting and seek to move beyond the impact of grace killing patterns of passive-aggressive cycles.

Women, who have struggled in covert (passive-aggressive), emotional relationships eventually become very frustrated as they experience wounds at the core of their hearts. Hope gets deferred due to lost of dreams, desires and unfulfilled expectations. If this tension of irritation, resentment and anger is not dealt with in a healthy way, bondages of bitterness will take root. Ladies, I encourage you to heal and release your emotions of anger and resentment. Your Abba Father will not shame you for feeling angry at your situation. So often you have felt powerless to change the circumstances. However, your Abba Father is concerned about the way anger is handled. He is concerned about the inroads the Enemy will have in your life, if you do not walk the journey of release and restoration.

There is a destiny which has been prepared before the foundations of the world. Proverbs 4: 5 encourages you to "get wisdom and understanding." Grief has a way of gripping hearts so you almost feel like you cannot breathe. Life as you once knew it or wanted it to look, is shattered into pieces. Christian women find it hard to give themselves permission to grieve. However, losses must be grieved before you can move forward in a healthy way.

Keep the following steps in mind when beginning the grief process:

- Know and define what personal triggers lead to hurt, resentment, anger and inner turmoil.
- Be aware when you feel people have "stepped on your last nerve."
- Listen to your self-talk and when negative feelings pop up in your mind, purpose to not dwell on them. Instead, choose a healthy path. For example, choose to pray, journal, read the Bible, set a healthy boundary or communicate with a safe person.
- Take a time out! Give yourself adequate time to assess the reason for your grief.
- Ask the Holy Spirit to help. Do not let wounds turn into bitterness which may lead to a stronghold. Any unhealed strongholds will progress to bondage. Bondages hold a person captive and imprisoned. Psalm 37:8 reminds us to, "*Stop being angry! Turn from your rage! Do not lose your temper, it only leads to harm.*"
- Ask the Holy Spirit to give you His inner peace, as you walk the journey of the grief process.

~ WALKING IN AND THROUGH
THE STAGES OF GRIEF ~

The following are common responses to losses throughout life. Part of the healing process is to admit the truth of relationships. Detachment is a necessary component in order to step out of the dance of passive aggression and see the truth. You must move through all the stages of grief, sometimes more than once, if you are to walk in freedom and victory. Additionally, you will grieve the dreams, hopes and expectations you once held dear.

When you go through the process of grieving you are hit with a myriad of emotions. Healing is not very linear. Sometimes you will go through various stages of grief all at once, as you recount some memory of your relationship. Yet, there are specific tasks which must be completed in each stage to complete the process. At times, triggers or memories can throw you off balance. Dear Ones, rest assured this is very normal. Knowledge is extremely important; otherwise the enemy waltzes in your life and seemingly sets up camp.

Whenever, we encounter losses in life, we have grief work awaiting us. Grieving is not an easy task, when passive aggression is involved. In fact, it will be one of the hardest things you will do in life. Grief doesn't simply disappear by itself. There are potential consequences when we do not work through the stages of grief. If you try to ignore, or bury the feelings, they will raise their head in some way at some point in your life. Journeying through grief brings change and teaches great personal lessons. People do not experience all of the stages exactly the same way. Once again, be aware that people do not go through the grief journey in a linear or logical order. If you stay too long in any stage and feel stuck, please reach out and seek professional assistance. The following are the most common stages of the grief process.

Stage 1: Shock ~ Denial ~ Numbness
Common Theme: "*I can't believe this is happening to me!*"

In this stage there is a feeling of being in a bad dream. People are dazed by the overwhelming feeling of powerlessness to change their reality. It has hit like an avalanche. There is shock about where you are in your relationship. When the shock starts to wear off, the truth of things sets in and numbness takes over. Women respond differently. Some sit in their favorite comfort chair and wander off in their mind; wishing for life to return to the way it used to be, before the "passive aggressive chaos" took over. Other women try to act "normal" outwardly, but internally, they are screaming in silence. Still others stay overly busy with running around, so they avoid thinking about the hurt.

Shock happens when a person can no longer avoid the reality. They cannot push their pain down anymore. I remember taking my grandchildren to a fun center for a celebration. One of the games involved taking a "hammer-like toy" to hit a clown that would pop up. At first there were only one or two clowns that would pop-up and it was manageable. Then all of a sudden, as soon as one clown was pushed down several others would pop up. This juggling act soon became exhaustive; much like attempting to handle all the things involved in a passive-aggressive relationship and attempting to maintain an appearance of normalcy.

There is an internal battle of the mind that occurs when you recount repetitive situations. In the silence of your mind you say, "It has been so good in our relationship lately. What happened the other day?" You remember the day the passive-aggressive person came home and was not talking to you. You know you have not done one thing to push a button. He doesn't say much, but you know there is something wrong. You feel things, but you walk around in a daze. Things are so crazy and there is no resolve, and therefore no closure to the tension. All you can do is mumble under your breath words like, "There must be something I am doing to create this distance." You fight and protest, acknowledging this might be emotional abuse.

You dare not speak these words out loud. Therein lies the battle. If you deny the truth, it is contrary to the actual reality. It is contrary to everything in your spirit.

The realization you have been compensating, denying and compromising has set in and now you feel emotionally numb. Quite frankly, you don't even recognize the person you have become while trying to keep the peace. However, the personal cost of not walking through the process is that our emotions are being to shut down. Detachment occurs, which helps to face the situation and function from day to day. However, prolonged shut down prevents you from identifying the truth and communicating honestly with the other person.

Stage 2: Hurt and Anger ~ Searching and Longing
Common Theme: *"Sometimes I feel so hurt and angry inside."*

It is common, during this stage, to hear your self asking, "Why can't we go back to happier days?" The life you envisioned has vanished, along with future expectations. There is a sense of yearning and searching to find an answer to fill the voids and holes of the relationship. This yearning desire is very normal and is often accompanied with some level of anger. Before women become angry, they go through phases of sadness and hopelessness. Women frequently feel anger as they become impacted by repetitive passive-aggressive patterns; especially if there are children involved. The passive aggressive influence on their children brings fear. Women begin attempting various methods to bring resolution of the destructive cycles, and yet, nothing seems to work beyond a temporary reprieve.

Ladies, the anger may also be directed towards yourself. For women, the hurt and anger may go inward and manifest outwardly, such as shopping, withdrawing, isolating, depression, or over eating. Of course, these are only temporary emotional solutions. It is important to release anger in healthy and appropriate ways. When we push hurt feelings down it can make us sick inside, but be expressed outwardly in unhealthy ways. Now is the time to choose to deal with your emotional or relational pain. One of the ways to acknowledge your hurt is to again journal your thoughts. The journaling tool gets the facts, truth and distortions out in the open. Ask The Holy Spirit to reveal the innermost parts of your heart and help you untangle the web of grief emotions.

Stage 3: Bargaining ~ Despair
Common Theme: *"Hey, Let's make a deal. What if...? I should have . . .?"*

Over long periods of time you realize nothing is the same. During this time you may have made promises to try and stop the hurt feelings. Many search for ways to prevent despair. When women move into an anger phase, if they do not heal from the disappointments and disillusionment, compromising and bargaining comes on the scene. Bargaining comes out in the form of fixing, rescuing, masking and enabling. If the dreams, desires and hopes are not met, women experiences despair; searching for something to bring relief. It is my prayer that in viewing the grief path, you can identify the phase you are in and make a decision to get better and not become bitter. You must also decide, "enough is enough." You will have to start with yourself first and identify your own unhealthy patterns.

The patterns women need to break are the cycles of excusing, fixing, rationalizing, rescuing and denying the realities in their relationships. You will have to ask the Holy Spirit to assist you in discerning what truth is, and what it is not. You will have to seek discernment to sort out what is fact, and what you may have altered, so you can survive the drama. Jehovah Rapha, the God that heals, can and will heal you. Seek Him and He will be found. When you are in this stage, and do not work it completely through, you might develop negative attitudes in the relationship, which can lead to depression.

Stage 4: Depression ~ Despair
Common Theme: *"What's the point"* or *"This is messed up!"*

A person can feel so sad and hopeless that it leads to depression. Women dealing with passive-aggressive people are worn down and exhausted. Depression can affect eating and sleeping habits. It can also impact how you feel about your identity and self-worth. You may have low energy and a belief will rise up which says, "I could care less what you are doing and where you are going." You do your own thing, because it is more peaceful than trying to engage in the relationship with a passive-aggressive man. This is not the blessing the Lord has for you. He does not desire you remain in depression. He desires that women speak the truth and live unshackled. *"But you belong to the Lord, my dear children. You have already won a victory over those people, because the Spirit who lives in you is greater than the spirit who lives in the world." (1John 4:4).* The Lord will be with you in this journey of healing.

Stage 5: Acceptance ~ Acknowledgment
Common Theme: *"I feel relieved. Internal Peace can be restored"*

In this stage, you learn to accept things as they are, and not as you would like them to be. This is an emotionally freeing phase. This is not a stage of resignation. On the contrary it is a time where you can celebrate that you have been able to step away from the entanglement of the passive-aggressive dance. You have begun to regain your identity and self value. You have emerged and you are now having moments and glimpses of seeing your new self. You gain the ability to weave your journey into a testimony. There is an acceptance of the reality of what has changed inside, so you can walk in maturity and health.

In working with people who have experienced various forms of loss, I have learned there are additional stages of the grief process which lead to redefining your life. As Christian women, keep in mind there is a component of spiritual warfare when pain, resentments and forgiveness are not fully processed or replaced with healthy behaviors and renewal of the mind. My sisters, rejoice and stand victorious as you continue your journey.

Stage 6: Re-investment ~ Reframing
Common Theme: *"Living Unshackled"*

Healing changes people because there is always growth involved. However, you must learn to walk as a new person who has been restored. Redefining identity comes with risks. You must step through the fears and take action anyway. Ladies, as you reframe your thinking and walk unshackled by your past, you will be learning to get back into the flow of life. You have persevered and are a new person. Revival and renewal of our innermost parts is accomplished in this stage of reframing. When you faithfully do the practical work of healing, the Lord will be faithful to do the supernatural in your life circumstances.

Take time, my sisters, and give thanks to the Lord for your victory. *"Precious Lord, I thank you for taking my hand, walking alongside and carrying me through this triumphant journey. I pray you will continue to give me courage and boldness to stand for the truth and win the emotional, relational and spiritual battles. I give you honor and praise you Lord for the strength you have given me and the ability to let go of. . ."*

Re-investment into life and reframing of thinking is a wonderful stage that rebuilds confidence and identity. Step by step, one day at a time, people begin to trust again. Women who get to this stage are clearly able to communicate appropriate boundaries in an honest fashion. The season of re-investing in life brings a sense of freedom.

~ MILESTONES OF A HEALTHY GRIEF JOURNEY ~

There are several milestones to evaluate and determine if you have walked through and completed a healthy grief journey. As you read through the list, check the areas you have completed. Why is it important to periodically review? First, this list will identify where you need to continue reframing for the future. Second, you can celebrate the accomplished victories.

- I have come face to face with the reality of my situation. I am committing to change the things I can, and letting go of what I cannot change. In doing so, I will gain serenity and freedom from strife.
- I have worked through the depth of pain. My hurt is no longer controlling my decisions and choices in an unhealthy way.
- I have stopped trying to fix, rescue and make excuses for the passive-aggressive person in my life.
- I am able to speak truth and accept responsibility for my own actions.
- I have decided to let goodness into my life again.
- I am able to find, and embrace, my identity in Christ, not in a role or another person.
- I have, or am learning to practice, self-care without guilt or shame. I know the difference of taking care of myself and being self-centered.
- I can identify emotional and physical signals such as: feelings of irritability, regrets, episodes of severe pain, inability to function on a daily basis, or disturbances in eating and sleeping patterns.
- I do not base my relationships entirely on trying to please the other people without expressing healthy boundaries.
- I no longer put myself down for being vulnerable.

Stage 7: Recognize Triggers ~
Common Theme: "Triggers do not mean I haven't let go"

Recognizing triggers of past behaviors, patterns and memories does not mean you have not healed. As humans, we do not forget, however, there is choice in how we respond. If you are triggered, discover the root and take appropriate steps to remain in freedom. So many times people struggle when they are triggered and there is an urge to go back to old styles of dealing with the drama or pain of the past. It is like the Israelites who wanted to go back to Egypt and God was trying to take them to the Promised Land. Ladies, keep taking one step at a time out of Egypt and head towards the Promised Land of freedom and do all you can to stay on the healing path. *Dear Ones do not go back to Egypt!* When you experience an emotional trigger, ask as soon as possible if you are being or feeling: rejected, attacked, threatened, or are currently dealing with internal turmoil.

Stage 8: Learn to Walk in New Skin ~
Common Theme: "This is a new day."

Ladies, when you come to this stage, it is truly about personal maturity. So you must see yourself differently. Transitioning when you are emotionally vulnerable is difficult. This stage is an unfolding of a healthy, restored identity which requires you to be ruthlessly honest with yourself. This is a time when all the pieces come together. The following are indicators that you have successfully grieved.

- Ability to use life's challenges as a path toward growth and maturity. As you mature you learn to deepen and strength relationships with God, self and others.
- Ability to find intentional purpose and destiny in the battles, which is a path to spiritual growth.
- Ability to live in the present, while using the past as knowledge to prevent sabotaging patterns from resurfacing.
- Ability to identify and live with realistic goals and desires.
- Ability to name passive-aggressive characteristics and know how and when to step out of the dance without hardening your heart.
- Ability to honestly state what you feel, and face the hurt without becoming defensive.
- Ability to select and connect to emotionally safe people. You have established accountability partners to help you stay the course while walking out the healing journey.

Stage 9: Staying in the Promised Land
Common Theme: "I have healthy boundaries."

As you are fully aware of by now, it is extremely important to maintain healthy boundaries with a passive-aggressive person. The more blurred boundaries become, the more you will be manipulated or entrapped, time and time again in the web and world of passive-aggression. Boundaries are limits set to honor you and another person without building resentments. Ladies, if you ignore setting healthy boundaries, you will pay a hefty price that will move you right out of the Promise land and back into a wilderness walk.

Stage 10: Stepping out of Prison
Common Theme: "Forgiveness, is a path to emotional, physical and spiritual health"

Ladies, it is very difficult to walk through the path of forgiveness when you have experienced long-term emotional abuse. The grace and mercy of God has given forgiveness to each of us, so we do not stay imprisoned in a jail cell of resentment and bitterness. Forgiveness allows you to walk out of bondage and captivity. It may seem impossible to you after all you have endured. I realize the acts of pain have been etched on your hearts. However, if you choose not to practice forgiveness, you may pay a high price. As you recall, the passive-aggressive person disperses chaos and pain and moves on, as though, nothing has happened. You are the one left slumped over and wounded. Whenever you embrace the Lord's grace to forgive, you are able to enter into a place of abiding peace, restoration, healing, hope and joy. I Thessalonians 5:24 says, "God will make it happen, for He who calls you is faithful."

If you do not feel you have the strength or desire to forgive, God will make a way. Remember forgiveness is a process, as well as, an act of obedience to the Heavenly Father. Basically, forgiveness is a divine design to allow you to grieve and let go of the right for revenge. I know some of you have wanted to go somewhere and scream at the top of your voices. The confusion and pain in your hearts lead to being emotionally mad; however, you got physically sick. *Can you relate!* The people, who have hurt you, will have to come face to face with themselves. Remember, forgiveness is about you being victoriously released from the prison of resentment and bitterness.

One very important emotion which may need resolving before you can completely let go, is bitterness. Bitterness is a frozen emotion which has become rooted as a result of unreleased losses. Additionally, it can grow from denial, rejection, followed by shock, guilt, anger, bargaining, and depression which are part of grieving. It can be the loss of hope, dreams, reputation, relationships, job and expectations. Bitterness is the result of consistently being hurt by a painful memory and a person is holding onto the hurt, until the loss has become a stronghold. The cause of the hurt can be words, attitudes and actions of others.

When you are offended or disappointed by others and allow the negative emotions to seep into your heart, bitterness and resentment will take root. If you do not grieve in a healthy way and dwell on the replay of hurt, then bitterness will constantly invade your thoughts. The mind will become a playground for inner turmoil. Bitterness is like having a deadly drink and hoping the other person dies. It is a slow way to destroy your peace of mind, which then becomes a spiritual warfare battle. We are responsible for what we do, say, think and feel. Bitterness is a trap the Enemy uses to move you into a sea of regret and despair. Unresolved bitterness, is frozen anger buried alive, and will eventually affect you emotionally, physically and spiritually. The antidote to bitterness is forgiveness.

The journey of forgiveness will take time. We first say, "Lord I know I need to forgive, but you know the bucket load of pain I am in right now. I do not know how I can release him! He hasn't even admitted his part in the painful events." This is the obedience part, which is taking it to the Lord in prayer and being honest about where you are in that moment! The process part is you will have to walk through the pain before you get to the other side of forgiveness.

I have discovered many in the faith-based communities have misconceptions about forgiveness. **Let's take some time and clear up some ideas on forgiving others and yourselves:**

- Forgiveness does not mean you deny, excuse, minimize, justify or rationalize the offender's responsibility in hurting you.
- Forgiveness is not a feeling. It is a choice and an act of will. Depending on the severity of an offense, forgiveness may be a journey that will be passed through many times.
- Forgiveness is an intentional commitment to the process of change and to step away from being a victim.
- Forgiveness may bring you an open door to show empathy and compassion for others.
- Forgiveness may require you to journal and reach out for help if you are emotionally stuck.
- Forgiveness does not always lead to reconciliation. Reconciliation may be a challenge or impossibility; if the offender has died, remains relationally toxic or is unwilling to communicate with you to bring healing.
- Forgiveness is not an automatic response when you have been attacked, abused, or betrayed. It will take accountability, support, prayer and a Holy Spirit intervention. My sisters, the truth is, it will also take many tears. I know you have been there!
- Forgiveness is about how you will be impacted if you don't, as well as, if you choose to forgive. My sisters, do not skip any step in the process of restoration. I encourage you to let go, release yourself and be set free from the stronghold of resentment and bitterness.

Stage 11: Seeking God's Face by Receiving Full Grace
Common Theme: Walking the Path of Restoration

- **Admit you have been hurt** ~ Let the Lord help you on the path of restoration. *"So humble yourselves under the mighty* power of the Lord, and at the right time He will lift you up in honor." (1 Peter 5:6)

- **Personal ownership** ~ Accept responsibility to grow and heal. *"We are each responsible for our own actions."* (Galatians 6:5)
- **Grieving** ~ Letting go, reframing and reinvesting into life is all part of transformation and restoration. *"The Lord comforts us in all of our troubles so that we can comfort others. When they are troubled, we will be able to give them the same comfort that the Lord has given us."* (2 Corinthians 1:4)

~ Prayer ~

"Heavenly Father, I come to you, recognizing that you are my healer and deliverer. When I have come to the end of my strength, I come to the beginning of Yours. I rejoice in declaring that you are omnipotent, omniscient, and omnipresent. You are merciful and are Adonai, Lord over all. You know where I am struggling and the things which are keeping me in a state of continuous grief. I have faith that you will restore my joy and hope. Amen"

Chapter 12

Satan's Inroads to Relationships ~

The Truth will set you Free

"Trust in the Lord with all your heart; do not depend on your own understanding. Seek His will in all you do, and He will show you which path to take." (Proverbs 3:5-6)

You shake your head, knowing there is more involved than meets the eye. Yes, as a counselor and conference speaker, I have seen many times when spiritual warfare is involved beyond what the people see. Therefore, I would be remiss if spiritual warfare was not addressed in how it impacts passive-aggressive relationships. It comes as no surprise that Satan, also known as the Enemy, attempts unprecedented attacks when our confidence is in a crisis. His goal is to immobilize and prevent you from taking positive action. However, with this information, you will again have the key to the kingdom principles to make life-changing growth decisions.

Once again in human history, the enemy of our souls is coming after the families through addictions, pornography, divorce, and domestic violence, and abuses of all kinds. We must become prepared and be familiar with the deceit of the enemy. Now, do not get me wrong, regardless of what the enemy, or other people do in our lives, we must still take ownership for how we deal with the drama, pain, hurt, rejection and betrayal from the circumstances.

Recognizing we are in a spiritual battle is the first step of boldly standing in the midst of adversity. Whenever you are entangled in passive-aggressive relationships, you will feel powerless in the battle to break free of oppression. My sisters, keep your focus and internal speech on the Lordship of Jesus in your life. By doing this, you will keep from being stuck in unhealthy patterns and negative thoughts.

If we declare what Jesus tells us in Matthew 28: 18, when He says, *"I have been given all authority in heaven and on the earth,"* then we realize the Lord has the authority and stands ready to help us. Spiritual warfare is defined as the battle waged in the unseen spiritual realm, which is revealed in the natural, physical realm. Implementing spiritual warfare tools is a proactive approach to releasing our faith in any circumstance. It will bring victory to your life as you gain greater understanding of the nature of spiritual warfare and its connection to passive aggression. As you gain clarity and apply warfare principles to your life, I guarantee you will move from feeling like a powerless victim, to standing firm in whatever battles you face, knowing you can live through them in triumph.

If you are a follower of Jesus, you have been given the gift of the Holy Spirit to meet you daily in whatever your situation. The Holy Spirit will guide, direct and empower you to know what to do when hit by the enemy. As you obtain increased knowledge and awareness, your thought life will become healthier and more ready for spiritual battles. The reality is, the Enemy will keep trying his tactics against you, but when you are confidently convinced of your spiritual authority he will continually lose. Your role is to boldly recognize, resist and reinstate your faith to let the Lord anoint you to fight the spiritual battle. The Lord will walk with you to bring victory. God's truth in addition to your relationship with Jesus Christ equals resistance to the enemy. For additional empowerment, I encourage you to read 1Peter 5:9

As princess warriors, you are to be alert to the schemes of the enemy. You are not to become fearful. Nor are you to live in a state of suspicion and paranoia about every life event. You do not need to go out of your way looking for demonic activity, but when you encounter it, you can learn to recognize it and boldly confront with the spiritual authority given by the Lord. Abuses of all forms must be dealt with intentionally and swiftly. The Bible tells us not be afraid and God will strengthen, help, and uphold us through all of life's adversities. Therefore, my sister now is not a time to be timid in proclaiming who you are in Christ Jesus. Seek God's face and continue to pursue an intimate walk with Him, so you become stronger during the healing path ahead.

Whenever you practice a walk of faith, God adds to your strength. Your renewed and enhanced strength builds transformation, courage, boldness and confidence in the spiritual battles you face. You may be disappointed, feeling burdened and overly stressed by the crazy-making cycles of passive aggression, but the Lord is ready to fortify and anoint you to walk it through. When you take steps in the Lord's name, faith moves miraculously in your life. To be free enough to reach for your full potential, is to be free indeed.

In this section, I will give you a few names and characteristics of the enemy of our souls as it relates to how the enemy uses passive aggression to bring about harmful relational outcomes. I'll also remind you, this list relates to passive-aggressive people and the battles they face as well. For a more complete understanding of spiritual warfare you may want to refer to my two previous books, *Standing Victoriously in the Battle*, and *Weapons to Stand Boldly and Win the Battle*. The first book is directed at women and the second is specifically for men. I encourage men and women to read both books for a full boarder view of spiritual warfare. For now, let's take a specific look at the inroads the Enemy uses to attempt our defeat relationally.

SPIRITUAL WARFARE ~ INROADS OF PASSIVE AGGRESSION

Ladies, be empowered as you unravel the correlation of how the enemy attacks relationships and families. There are deliberate strategies used by the Enemy to entrap and separate humans from God while bringing disunity and destruction in their relationships. We cannot afford to make the mistake of thinking we are not in a strategic war. However, the Enemy does shudder when we walk in the light of truth and reality. We can learn a lot about how the Enemy of our soul began to hit and bring separation of relationships in the bible. The first form of passive aggression can be seen in the book of Genesis as we view what occurred in the Garden of Eden between Adam and Eve. The first human relationship became relationally broken by the influence of enemy tactics.

The Garden of Eden ~ Chaos and Disunity Unleashed

In the Garden of Eden, Satan appeared as a serpent to Eve. The strategic tactic the enemy used was one of deceptive enticement, shame, blame, division and temptation. The enemy attempted to destroy the warrior man and the priestly mantle of the masculine soul. Satan was able to immobilize Adam through passivity. Satan convinced Eve to doubt the truth; disobey God and eat the fruit from the tree of knowledge of good and evil. He deceitfully enticed Eve by distorting God's words and insinuating uncertainty about the characteristics of her Abba Father, God. In Genesis 3:1, the Enemy distorted God's instruction by asking Eve, ". . . *Did God really say that you must not eat the fruit from any of the trees in the garden?"* From then, to this day, if we have distorted beliefs about the Lord, it is an inroad from the Enemy to mess with our heart and mind. That is why, part of healing and transformation will require the renewing of your mind. We must take a personal inventory of our behavior and choices and take ownership, so we can move forward to a path of freedom. Passive aggression fosters an environment of fear, shame and doubt in self, others and God. In the Garden of Eden, the serpent's tactic was to have Eve believe God was withholding knowledge, wisdom and truth. The Enemy's tactics may involve muddling of your mind, creating confusion and disorder.

Satan also utilized the tactic of divisiveness in the Garden of Eden. Adam passively stood by and watched Eve go against instructions given to them by the Lord. He did not protect her in a priestly way, as God had directed. As you know, after Eve and then Adam ate the fruit, their eyes were opened to the knowledge of good and evil. When God came to visit them and called their names, they were both afraid and hid. Women today who are in abusive relationships also hide the truth of what is happening in their lives, regardless whether the patterns are being felt at work, home, family, friends or church environments. Women particularly will hide or cover the truth in significant personal and professional relationships. In the book of Genesis chapter three, we see the plans of Satan unfold. When God questioned Adam as to what had happened, for the first time, blame and shame entered the world. After God confronts Adam, he becomes aggressive and begins to boldly blame God for giving him the woman, and then he blames Eve. When Eve hears what Adam says, she protects herself by blaming the serpent. There is a whole lot of blaming and shaming going on in this scenario. Can you relate to Eve and Adam?

As women, can you envision what Eve felt after having experienced a sweet, truthful, open relationship with God and her husband, Adam? All of a sudden, aggressive accusations hit her, which went deep into the core of her heart. Can you picture how that woman must have dropped her head in shame before God and her husband? She might have dealt with a sick sinking feeling in the pit of her stomach. I dare say, at the very least, she probably experienced emotions of betrayal, rejection, mistrust, guilt and fear. This struggle between men and women continues to this day. There was both passivity and aggression in the responses of Adam. There was passivity on the part of Eve. My sister, as you read on, look for the insights in correlating the schemes of Satan in the Garden and Eden and the ways he could capitalize on the passive-aggressive tendencies today. The Enemy does not use different tactics today. The intent is divisiveness through deception.

When we speak about how the Enemy uses the passive-aggressive person, three names of the Enemy come to the forefront. These three descriptive names and associated tactics demonstrate the strategy the enemy implements to infiltrate the mind of the passive-aggressive person. The first name we are going to view is *The Slanderer*.

The Slanderer ~ Identity Thief

Satan's Trait: The Slanderer is an enemy who passes judgment on personal identity. He attempts to have men live a veiled lifestyle. Satan wants you to believe you are nothing to God and it is not possible to change. He wants humans to retain their distorted images of God, therefore discounting who they really are in Christ.
God's Redemptive Truth: Your identity is in Christ. He created your inmost being. He does not want you to experience any voids in your heart, due to unmet needs by other human beings. He knit you together in your mother's womb. You are wonderfully made.

Have you ever had someone attack your personhood? Has anyone tried to slander your name by berating your character, through shame, or piling on false guilt? Has it created inner turmoil? If so, then it is time to step into victory. The passive-aggressive person struggles with an identity problem of not feeling secure, and therefore is very vulnerable to the wiles of the enemy. When you know the root of your insecurity, you can determine to heal and stop the enemy. Otherwise, He will attempt to immobilize you in being triumphant in your personal or professional journey.

Men, who have experienced this enemy tactic of "identity thief," in the earlier years of their lives, must go deep and uncover the seeds of distortions in their lives. Otherwise, various forms of dealing with or numbing out their pain will take root. Passive-aggressive patterns are one of the ways of dealing with their anger, hurt, rejection and emotional disconnection. The men, who are struggling with unresolved pain, need to know there is no shame in asking for help to be set free. The distortions of themselves, others and God are robbers for the passive-aggressive man. The second name of the Enemy which gives an understanding of the correlation between spiritual warfare and passive aggression is ***Abaddon***.

Abaddon ~ Destroyer of Relationships

Satan's Trait: The enemy will try to destroy you, or render you relationally ineffective in this world.
God's Redemptive Truth: God promises a redemptive path is available to you. There is a destiny beyond yourself and forgiveness for the mistakes of the past as you walk new battleground.

"**Abaddon**" literally means destroyer and destruction. Revelations 9:11 refers to Satan with this terminology. Take a moment and visualize an army getting ready for battle. The whole idea of preparing for battle is to destroy the enemy. The Enemy's groundwork is to prepare for battle and bring about our destruction. Satan will do anything to see us destroyed or become defenseless, so his army can continue to rob, steal and destroy. Abaddon will use family, friends, jobs, ministry, past mistakes, and past pain to bring people down. In passive-aggressive relationships, most issues are never resolved or healed. If there is no healing or learning to grieve and forgive, the Enemy, Abaddon, will resurrect these issues. These unresolved areas become places of an inroad for the enemy because the issues of the past keep resurfacing in the future. Many times, a person will begin to speak negatively about hurtful unresolved issues. The negative self-talk will continue to replay the past to destroy your present and influence your future.

Whether it is the process of destroying or the result of complete destruction, Abaddon has the goal of rendering everyone unproductive for the Kingdom of God. What greater way of doing this, than to strike the infrastructure of a family, a ministry or an organization. The use of these tactics serves to abort the destiny God planned for individuals since the beginning of time. Satan desires to incapacitate people who rise-up and connect with Abba Father. The final Enemy name we will look at as it relates to passive-aggressive relationships is *Beelzebub*.

Beelzebub ~ Preying on Hurts and Wounds

Satan's Trait: Beelzebub will feed off anything open wound. Beelzebub wants you to believe that if you have weakness, insecurity or hurts, you are destined to remain a victim.
God's Redemptive Truth: Jehovah Rapha, God who Heals, is able to heal and redeem you. He is able to heal you emotionally, spiritually and relationally.

When the Pharisees in Matthew 12:24 accused Jesus of driving out demons by the power of Satan called Beelzebub, it is the first time the name is used in the Bible. Beelzebub literally means the Lord of the Flies and prince of the fallen angels, called demons.

This reference to Satan makes sense when we consider how flies swarm, and feed off dead things. Beelzebub attempts to feed off the dead, or painful, things in your life. These dead things shoot up from prior events. If there is a focus on the past, it affects existing choices. If the Enemy feasts on places of wounds, imperfections or shame, we potentially develop a distorted belief system that threatens to hinder intimacy in significant relationships. Often the passive-aggressive person is triggered when they feel threatened. As they recount their past hurts, it is easy to obstruct the very thing they desire, which is connecting and bonding.

I have observed people living a merry-go-round lifestyle. They continue to use futile methods expecting different outcomes. Unhealed painful experiences can cause people to spiral until they develop *inner promises*, which are *inner protective vows*. If they do not stop spiraling and heal the root issues which created these inner vows, the enemy, Beelzebub, will use it. For example, people make inner vows such as: *"I will never let anyone get too close to me again," "I will never be weak or powerless in the future,"* or *"I will never need anyone."* When inner vows take hold, they create an internal prison cell.

The Enemy feeds off people who hold onto areas of weakness, hurt, insecurity or shame-based thinking. This enemy does not want you to acknowledge negative thinking patterns and flaws. Psalm 34:19 tells us we have many afflictions in life. The Lord will deliver us from those afflictions and set us free. To find freedom, you must speak the truth, stand on the Word, and declare and live the truth out, as you walk through the healing process. When our mind is filled with doubt, it cannot focus on the path of victory.

~ Prayer ~

"Heavenly Father, I want to thank you for lifting me up out of despair and disappointment. I realize as your daughter you are setting my feet on solid ground. Thank you for remaining close to me in this journey. I am praying and singing a halleluiah victory song as I continue to break into the world of passive aggression, break out with equipping tools, and finally receive my breakthrough." Selah.

Chapter 13

Freedom from Powerless Pain ~
Victory is yours to Declare

"Keep putting into practice all you have learned and received from me; everything you heard and saw me doing. Then the God of peace will be with you." (Philippians 4:9)

It is not a coincidence that you are reading this book at this appointed time. Dear Ones, you do not need to remain powerless and immobilized. Keep your faith ignited by fanning the flame of hope. However, continue to gain wisdom and tools to live in triumph. Part of obtaining that wisdom will involve some introspection and retrospective insight. The healing journey involves coming face to face with yourself and owning your personhood and making intentional changes in your life. As you unveil personal patterns and learn to set healthy boundaries, it will bring freedom and sanity in any of your passive-aggressive relationships. There are times, when a woman in the faith-based community struggles with retaining a place of personal freedom.

Continual tension becomes a struggle for Christian women who are connected with passive-aggressive men. They try to walk a Christ-centered life while being personally challenged to set healthy boundaries. Yet, these same women, who often desire a life of integrity, wind up living masked lives in an attempt to cover the *silent cry of pain*. These women cannot resolve their experience of personal isolation, rejection, grief and hurt in their own lives with what they view as living a healthy "Christian women."

Throughout history and in various people groups, the meaning of submission has been taken far from God's plan. Because of this, it has left a bitter taste for many women. Unfortunately, in various denominations, people have used the term submission to get women to conform through control. This historical confusion creates a negative societal message and women living with passive-aggression relationships often cringe when the word submission is mentioned. I am fully convinced God did not mean for this word to be used the way in which many faith-based communities have defined it today.

Sadly, many women have experienced the unhealthy and ungodly meaning of the word submission and surrender. They have heard something along the lines, *"The problems with your husband are because you have not been compliant, submissive or walked in total obedience."* Other women have shared when they went to church to have someone facilitate a healing process; they were criticized and told, *"You must have provoked him."* Seemingly, the church saw the man as being kind and the woman as being too strong. When you are dealing with passive aggression, it is difficult for the world to see the behavioral patterns, especially since the cycles include presenting a mask to the world and an entirely different one in private.

Christian women married to non-believers, might submit in an unhealthy manner because they believe it will win their husbands into the kingdom. Women married to Christian passive-aggressive men, are constantly doubting their walk with the Lord and second-guessing their own motives. Eventually, they lose their focus and identity because they continually compromise their beliefs in order to *keep the peace*. The self-talk becomes a message which goes something like, *"It's better to give-in and prevent the drama."* They think they are being Christ-like and serving, as unto God, by totally surrendering and deferring to the man's leadership, even in the face of unbiblical behaviors. This thinking creates a multitude of future problems, while setting a precedent for unhealthy behavioral patterns.

Women, who begin to compromise truth and reality, consistently give false permission to the passive-aggressive person to continue with the same destructive emotional and verbal patterns. I know this statement is hard to read as Christian women. I can guess some of you are thinking, doesn't the Bible say the man is to be the spiritual head in the home. Yes, it does. However, submission never authorizes any form of abuse. It is not demanded, nor should it produce fear, shame, manipulation, intimidation or control.

In Matthew 12:35 it says, *"A good person produces good things from the treasury of a good heart, and an evil person produces evil things from the treasury of an evil heart."* The hostility stored in a person's soul will rise in that person's life. In your attempt to prevent further hurt and pain, you have learned a set of behavioral patterns which enable the destructive cycles to persist. Dear Ones, this book is intended to break the silence of abuse, give knowledge, so you can get off the emotional merry-go-round and reunite with your true identity and destiny. The Enemy of our souls will use covert (hidden) abuse to eradicate dreams and hopes. So many times, the thing which drives women to stay with passive-aggressive men is the *compassion for the boyishness* of these men.

Often, women feel they can make a difference and somehow help the men. Some women focus on believing they are making a Christian choice and so the cycle of abuse continues undetected. They begin blaming themselves when their marriages or relational connections do not bring closeness or unity. The distorted belief of some women, says, *"I chose to marry this man and now, I must make the best of the situation and be submissive."* Out of inadequate knowledge, the faith-based community has done an injustice to women in abusive situations.

The Lord promises He has a future and a destiny planned out for you. *"For I know the plans I have for you, says the Lord. They are*

plans for good and not for disaster, to give you a future and a hope."
(Jeremiah 29:11) Destiny implies a path towards a destination.
Destination incorporates an intentional process and a chosen journey
a person travels to fulfill that destiny. Your Abba Father has heard
the silent cry of His daughter, and He desires to give you hope and
courage to walk your personal path with your identity fully intact.
He desires that you walk empowered by Him in your spiritual gifts,
exercising your talents and releasing your fullest potential. He has
not forgotten you! Although it may feel that way at times, be assured
you are held in the palm of His hand. **I pray the Holy Spirit directs
your path to wholeness, freedom. For a believer, freedom means:**

- You are liberated to choose the path of freedom.
- You are unbound, in order to forgive and receive forgiveness.
- You are free to let others disagree and not try to fix, rescue, or
  enable them.
- You are strengthened to stand boldly in passive-aggressive
  environments.
- You are delivered to live with enthusiasm and passion, instead
  of performing for approval, because you know who you are in
  Christ.
- You are released to deal with the realities of life and take owner-
  ship for your choices.
- You are unhampered and able to set healthy boundaries when
  appropriate.
- You are unhindered to live your divinely given purpose with
  limitless possibilities.

***Power Tool**: "*Although you may not see yourself as having the
gift of freedom. The Lord is working out the details of your circumstances, even as you read, so mark this page. Use this list to identify
areas you desire and don't feel you have yet. If you struggle with any
of these statements, begin praying for the free gift that is listed. In
doing so, it will give you a starting place to address the reasons for
any lack of freedom in your life.*"

I thank the heavenly Father for the grace He wants to pour out to you. The Lord's grace is like a robe that covers you with peace, faith, perseverance, and joy. The Lord is able to restore you physically, spiritually and emotionally. He will restore your sanity! Declare it and then hold your head up and give Him praise. I pray you stand victoriously in the arms of the Lord's grace and love for you. The Lord is working out the details of your circumstances, even as you read these pages.

The King of Glory will come to help you through the valley. Just as Moses followed God's plan and crossed the Red Sea onto dry land, you are also able to pass through challenging situations and remain in God's loving protection. Trust Him by applying truth and replacing distortions and Satan's lies. With God's truth, you will also more quickly realize the potential traits and tendencies of passive-aggressive people and those wrapped in the chaos. I also know this is a complicated process, especially, if you are experiencing brokenness in spirit and heart. It will take time and being intentional to walk through the process. You can be set free internally and fulfill your divine called purpose, unencumbered by pain, hurt and rejection. *There has never been the slightest doubt in my mind that the Lord, who began a great work in you, will bring it to a flourishing finish.* The Lord will keep intervening by imparting truth and wisdom, if you seek Him and let him come into the center of your pain.

As I stated previously, you have an enemy, named Satan, who has maximized strategic tactics to kill the spirit, hope, peace, dreams and visions of women. Throughout history he has thrived on those living in chaotic and abusive environments. Understand the truth that you are fighting an enemy who is incapable of showing grace or mercy. The enemy will use people to be grace killers. Grace killers are people who attack, shame, neglect or reject people around them in order not to be exposed for their own insecurities and fears. I encourage you to declare that the Lord's grace will step over circumstances and allow you to be a conqueror. The Enemy will attempt to keep you in an agitated state of confusion and hopelessness. The truth is the Lord has imparted several spiritual principles we can declare and stand upon with confidence.

The word grace is utilized by people of faith to mean *God's riches at Christ's expense*. Years ago, the Holy Spirit gave me another **GRACE** acronym, which goes like this: **G**od will **R**edeem **A**ll **C**haos for **E**ternal purposes. Whatever chaos is in your life, you have a redeemer, who will walk alongside you. Freedom and victory is possible!

~ DECLARE and STAND BOLDLY ~

- **We can stand on the precious name of the Lord**. *"Only by your power can we push back our enemies; only in your name can we trample our foes."* Psalm 44:5

- **We can stand confidently on the Word of the Almighty God**. *"Look, I have given you authority over all the power of the enemy and you can walk among snakes and scorpions and crush them. Nothing will injure you."* Luke 10:19

- **We can believe in the power of the Holy Spirit**. *"But you belong to the Lord, my dear children. You have already won a victory over people, because the Spirit who lives in you is greater than the spirit who lives in the world."* 1 John 4:4

- **We can put our trust and mustard-seed sized faith in Jesus**. *". . . Hold up the shield of faith to stop the fiery arrows of the enemy."* Ephesians 6:16

*Power Tool: *"The Lord values you by promising to give you His divine support. How marvelous is that? Take the above precious promises and use them as a tool, so that you walk through the healing journey with courage, victory and boldness with the Word as your spiritual weapon."*

~ ARMORED WITH VICTORY WEAPONS ~

Well, you have come a long way by persevering through the book. Now, you know how to use the tools you've examined. You are journaling, setting boundaries, communicating clearly and more easily identifying triggers in dealing healthily with the passive-aggressive person. Also, you have already looked at the attempts of the Enemy to diffuse successes and sabotage your relationships. You have what it takes to be strong within spiritual warfare. You are growing stronger and emotionally thriving every day. *Can you feel the cloud and fog lifting more each day?* Now, let's take a look at how to remain battle ready by taking up the armor of God. The battle with the Enemy is one you are already equipped to win. It is extremely essential to grasp how the Enemy of our soul seeks to weaken us when we walk in victory from passive-aggressive environments.

Satan is a schemer, who plans his strategic attack in areas of our vulnerability. He seeks the times of adversity, pain or hopelessness in order to find days of weakness and oppression. Walking in the shadows of denial or darkness is an inroad for the enemy. When you think of the spiritual meaning of darkness, it speaks to fear, blindness, hiding, cover-up, danger, and divisiveness. The list could go on and on. Spiritual victory weapons are designed to tear down the tactics of the enemy, while preventing strongholds from taking root in our lives. The Lord asks us to set out our spiritual warfare wardrobe, put it on, stand up and hold our ground.

Ephesians 6:1 tunes in to the fact that the enemy of our souls will wait patiently for opportune times to attack us. In this passage, Paul encourages you to, ". . . put on every piece of the Lord's armor so you will be able to resist the enemy. . ." The enemy will wait while the seeds of fear, shame and despair take root. He will cultivate the seeds in your mind and watch it come to full harvest. These germinated seeds can lead to strongholds and bondages. Then when the time of harvest is in the right season, Satan makes a strategic and tactical move. Sisters, do not be caught unaware of the Enemy and his tactics in your life. Make it personal!

The attire of the armor includes the belt of truth, breastplate of righteousness, shoes of peace, shield of faith, helmet of salvation and sword of the Spirit, which is the Word of the Lord. The character traits of truth, righteousness, peacefulness and faith will also make you stronger and more regal. Ask the Lord to search your heart, and reveal anything, which could be a hindrance to walking a life of freedom. **The very act of asking the Lord to expose any blind spots is a spiritual warfare winner.** This brings you out of darkness and into the light. God has declared your victory, and now you are to walk the journey armored for such a time as this.

Now, examine with me each powerful piece of the armor. It is necessary to be spiritually clothed when you step into the world each day. As you navigate the minefields of a passive aggression you must be proactive to be victorious in the battle. Our Heavenly Father never intends for you to fight and stand unarmed. The most significant understanding is that the human mind is the main battlefield chosen by the enemy. Yes, the battle of the mind, as outlined in the book of Ephesians, traps people.

The good news is the Lord has spiritual warfare weapons which don't change with the seasons and can continuously empower you to stand strong in the battle. You can confidently put on the full armor of the Lord. It is always in season, always in style and was created to fit you perfectly. The Bible tells us in the book of Ephesians chapter six to, *"Put on the full armor of God, so that when the day of evil comes, you may be able to stand your ground, and after you have done everything to stand. Stand firm..."* So, stand firm, my sisters.

God's Armor and Weapon: *Belt of Truth*
Satan's Counterfeit Armor: *Belt of Lies and Deception*
The Belt of Truth prepares you for action as seen in First Samuel 25:13. If truth is first, it holds everything else in place and is a foundational cornerstone. This piece of the armor reminds us to walk

in integrity by walking the truth. The best way to apply the Belt of Truth in your life is to continually ask yourself the following questions and answer honestly with prayer:

- Am I truthful with myself when I pray? Am I holding anything back from Father God?
- Am I allowing the Father of Lies to convince me of false beliefs or shameful thoughts?
- Am I allowing resentment or bitterness to remain in my heart and mind?
- Am I compromising any area of my life or moving my boundaries to please others?
- Have I been completely honest in answering the above questions?

God's Armor and Weapon: *Breastplate of Righteousness*
Satan's Counterfeit Armor: *Cloaks a heart that is unrighteous*

Sisters, as you put on the breastplate of righteousness, Proverbs 4:23 says to keep your heart pure with all vigilance, for out of it flows springs of life. Therefore, walk freely in fellowship with the Lord. Be specific when you put on this spiritual armor. Ask God to search your heart and fully reveal any area where the enemy can potentially weaken you. There are times, when you deal with passive aggression that you will feel, your anger is just and righteous. Keep in mind that even righteous anger, if unchecked, may lead to a path of unrighteousness. The anger may turn to resentment, leading to bitterness and then if left unhealed, will become a stronghold. Strongholds are prime entry places for the Enemy.

For those of you who did not have role models growing up, let Jesus be your example. He was the greatest man who exhibited upright character and righteous living. He was able to be empathetic, and yet he was a man of strength. Claim and believe you are made righteous in God's eyes because of the death and resurrection of His son, Jesus Christ. God is able to make you a conqueror over the enemy's attacks. 1 John 4:4 assures that, "Greater is He who is in you, than he who is in the world."

God's Armor and Weapon: *Gospel Shoes of peace*
Satan's Counterfeit Armor: *Spreads discontent, discord and distance from God and others*

Picture, a soldier's feet in combat boots. When a soldier is deployed to fight in a battle, he must wear the correct shoes. He intentionally wears combat boots instead of polished inspection shoes. Soldiers confidently choose the precise shoes to fit the assignment. You wouldn't wear high heels to play in a soccer tournament. Therefore, you understand, you must choose to wear the correct shoes. As effective soldiers in God's army, you must march over the thorny ground of enemy territory. The Bible speaks to you about shoes being part of the spiritual armor of God. He tells you to put on the "Gospel Shoes of Peace." It's a good time to ask yourself about where you choose to walk. Does your walk bring peace to the lives of those around you? The enemy wants you to believe that your offenses and wounds are grounds for maintaining relational distance with others. Of course, if you are dealing with toxic people, you must establish healthy boundaries. The enemy will raise a cloud of conflict to promote divisiveness. The intent of discord is a tactic by Satan to keep you from knowing God's peace with others and within yourself. God promises, as His daughter, you can have His peace in all situations. Remember, peace is not based on how you feel, but on what you know is truth.

Offensively, Jehovah Shalom's peace will equip you to stand with your feet firmly planted on His Word. If you stay planted, you will be unshaken by the enemy's threats and lies. It will protect you to keep steady when you are confronted by a passive-aggressive person. We need to know there is peace where we walk, and we need to be ready to leave that place if we are unsafe.

God's Armor and Weapon: *Helmet of Salvation*
Satan's Counterfeit Armor: *Blinds people to the need for Father God's salvation*

Hats have an interesting history and always make a statement of some kind. The Helmet of Salvation is strong and protects the soldier's head during battle. It gives you eternal perspective so your mind is able to make lasting choices rather than decisions that fit merely the day. First Corinthians 2:16 says we have the mind of Christ. Remember, the greatest battlefield is the mind. That is precisely why you must expose areas of possible "*stinking thinking.*" You know the resentment and bitterness that can creep into thinking over events such as a missed family time or unjust accusations. Those are the areas Satan potentially uses to inflict a fatal blow in the battles of life. However, the helmet of salvation allows you to guard your minds from fearful thinking, doubts and discouragement while you pray for clear focus.

Satan will constantly attempt to remind you of failures, past relational wounds and negativity in order to destroy your trust in God. Paul gives a solid weapon for victory in Philippians 4:8, where he tells us to focus on things that are true, pure, and lovely, of good report and value. Guard what you let enter into your mind. Do not let the Enemy lower your standards with thoughts like; "You should not get your hopes up. It will not work out anyway." As you immerse yourself in God's Word and prayer, you will develop a discerning mind, which unveils the enemy's subtle tactics.

Historically, helmets bore an insignia to identify with which army the soldier fought. This symbol would allow others quickly to identify friend or foe. You must protect your mind and thoughts while knowing what team you represent. The Word tells us, "We receive divine and mighty power to demolish strongholds and everything that sets itself up against the knowledge of God, and we can take captive every thought which causes us to walk out of God's will." The promise means you can sift and examine your thoughts in light of the Word.

God's Armor and Weapon: *Shield of Faith*
Satan's counterfeit Armor: *Fiery darts causing destruction and distraction*

In battle, shields obviously protect soldiers from fiery darts and sharp weapons. Currently, the shield of legal officers also helps identify who is serving to protect within society. Additionally, the

Shield of Faith gives us confidence that God will be on the front lines and His character is steady. We can have faith the Lord allows interception of many darts and arrows before they have a chance to penetrate. Remember, Satan's fiery arrows are meant to cause you to be distracted, stumble and ultimately to push you back. Without faith, the clever enemy will launch fiery darts to keep you from fulfilling the Lord's plans in your life. Being a follower of Jesus allows you to claim victory and use daily weapons to stand forthright with the passive-aggressive person.

God's Armor and Weapon: *Sword of the Spirit*
Satan's counterfeit Armor: *Poisons, twists, distorts and embellishes God's Word*

Currently, most women carry purses rather than swords. However, we can understand how historically the sword would serve to cut the enemy down during battle. In Ephesians, the Sword of the Spirit is referred to as the Word of God. Our sword is to speak the Word in faith. The Sword of the Spirit serves to defend and offensively attack the Enemy by slicing through his lies, so we can rightly define the truth. As we know, truth is essential in dealing with a passive-aggressive person. The Sword of the Spirit is one of the most powerful spiritual warfare weapons because it is capable of piercing the darkness of the Enemy. The sword accurately pinpoints what is happening in our lives. When you come face to face with the Adversary or Father of Lies, the Word of God is the only weapon capable of rendering him powerless. Prepare and protect your mind with the truth of God's word. Be assured, the Holy Spirit will guide you. Jesus, in the wilderness consistently used The Sword of the Spirit, when tempted by Satan. Each time Satan came to attack, Jesus stated, "It is written . . ."

Your Sword of the Spirit includes both the power of the Word and the name of Jesus Christ. You will notice there was no armor piece to protect your back. I believe it is because God has always "got your back." Sisters, in addition to the Armor of God, I have identified added weapons you can use to stand boldly and win in the daily battles.

Victory Weapon ~ Faith

In times of struggles, putting on the shield of faith will help you to stand firm and confident. *"Faith is the confidence that what we hope for will actually happen, it gives us assurance about things we cannot see,"* Hebrews 11:1-2. As we grow in our faith we understand that God is always ready, willing and able to fulfill his promises of freedom and rest. Sisters, there's only one thing stops him, your own disbelief or lack of faith. *"Now all glory to God, who is able, through His mighty power at work within us, to accomplish infinitely more than we might ask or think,"* Ephesians 3:12.

Victory Weapons ~ Prayer and Petition

Prayer is a distinct proactive weapon in facing life's issues. It prevents us from being apathetic. We don't need to wait around for the next shoe to drop. Actively seeking empowerment to face reality is being proactive. Sisters, pray as you start the healing process, pray during the journey and praise when you receive a breakthrough. Prayer breaks the strongholds, which keep us bound up. As you pray, ask the Lord to specifically enter into your process. Prayer ushers you into the presence of God and opens the heart to a deepening relationship with Him. Also, as prayers are answered people build a victory history with the Heavenly Father.

This historical understanding of your personal victory with the Lord allows for sustained boldness whenever the next trial, tribulation or enemy attack is fired in your direction. Know this my sisters, the Enemy will most assuredly attempt to immobilize you with thoughts such as, "This armor thing works for other people, but it hasn't worked for me" or "I do not know how to pray right." I encourage you to use the tools you have learned so far in this book. Pray specifically, intentionally and powerfully. *"Lord, I pray that you allow me to recognize when I am minimizing and excusing passive-aggressive cycles."* That is much stronger than saying, "Lord, help me know when not to repeat my same behaviors." I encourage you to pray the scriptures and be strengthened with each word.

One of my favorites is from Ephesians 3:20-21. *"Now all glory to God, who is able, through His mighty power to work within us, to accomplish infinitely more than we might ask or think. Glory to him in the church and in Christ Jesus through all generations forever and ever! Amen"*

Victory Weapon ~ Intimacy

Next, you must be aware of the ability to reach victory by spending quality and intimate time with the Lord. Time is a powerful weapon. The Enemy attempts to keep you occupied with many things. While the things in-and-of-themselves may not be bad, God's chief empowerment for you is released as you spend intimate time with Him. He makes the most of your time because He is the author of time. He then provides the things that fully benefit you. Making room for the Lord means you are filled daily with the Holy Spirit who teaches you to walk in the light.

Victory Weapon ~ Spiritual Alertness

Paul also highlights the awareness of being vigilant and alert. In 2006, I experienced a severe injury while ministering in Central Asia. After eight months without driving, I had to gain confidence to get behind the steering wheel again. Not only that, but developing alertness became a priority. I was painfully aware that without honed skills of alertness, I could endanger my life, as well as others on the road. This example powerfully illustrates how you must be alert, to steer the right direction and avoid the tactical schemes of the enemy. It's imperative you recognize who he is and what he is capable of doing in your life. John 10:10, reminds us Satan's purpose to rob, steal and destroy anything which brings glory to God. When you are intimately familiar with God's truth and promises, then any storms which come your way will be handled securely.

Victory Weapon ~ Perseverance

As you have continued reading in this book, you are persevering through hefty material and examining your own relationship with your Heavenly Father. Likely, you have become acutely aware of the Enemy's tactics in passive-aggressive relationships. This is proof you have an understanding of perseverance. This is a powerful weapon because it means you are able to intentionally take steps to stand. Satan, will defend what he believes belongs to him; mankind. However, the Lord is stronger than the Enemy. Ladies, you are already persevering and staying consistent in walking through the healing process with passive-aggressive and chaotic relationships.

Victory Weapon ~Worship

One of the most treasured and essential victory weapons is worship. I must say that when the Holy Spirit captivates our hearts, it is a joy to worship. Worship is an awesome and unusual weapon as it flows from a heart who sits in the presence of the Lord. Dear ones, as you become a person who worships, you will not seek to receive something from Him. The only heart desire when worshipping will be to bask in His presence and feel the Holiness of His love surrounding you. As you become a worshipper, you will solidify in your own heart and mind that you are a beloved daughter, with a heavenly inheritance. When you live a worship-filled life, no matter what season of adversity you are experiencing, you will not feel abandoned. Worship will keep your heart, mind and soul in a resting and trusting place with the Lord to supernaturally fight when you cannot battle for yourself.

As you mature as a worshiper, you realize there are different stages of worshiping and exercising your faith. When circumstances occur in your life, there are times it seems God is not near. I have learned to practice the presence of God and worship Him, regardless of how the circumstances make me feel. I will never forget the day, after returning from Central Asia with so much pain and bodily injury, that I attempted to get up from the bed and all I could do was fall back on it and cry out, *"Holy is your name, Oh Lord, my God and My Redeemer."* In the midst of crying out for help, I said, *"Jehovah Rapha if you do not show up and give me a fresh revelation of your holiness, I can't make it."* Beloved sisters, do not be afraid to admit when you feel powerless and need help. The greatest aid comes from the Lord. Even if you think things are not panning out the way you thought, faithfully believe the Holy Spirit is working it all out for you. His path is the perfect path for you.

Worship is about exalting the Lord. During worship, in the presence of Abba Father, bondages are broken, mindsets are straightened and hearts are healed. If you are not sure how to begin to worship, you can say something similar to the following:

"Abba Father, I magnify your name, because you are Holy. You are worthy, Oh Lord. You are My Jehovah Jireh, my Provider. You are my strong tower. Almighty God, I give you the glory and the praise. You are my Deliverer, in whom I can trust with my life and my family. You are my all and all." This illustrates the intimacy that develops with your Abba Father. Be real!

Victory Weapon ~ God's Precious Promises

The Lord promises to give us strength, wisdom, peace, comfort, hope, truth, grace and love. His Word is one of encouragement and endearment. When you come face to face with trials, tribulations, uncertainty or despair; remember there are precious promises from the Lord's Word you can claim and declare. Let these precious promises renew, restore and revive you. Let them speak life to your mind, heart and spirit!

"Do not be afraid, for I am with you. Do not be discouraged, for I am your Abba Father. I will strengthen you and help you. I will hold you up with my victorious right hand." ~ Isaiah 41:10

"The Lord keeps you from all harm and watches over your life. The Lord will keep watch over you as you come and go, both now and forever." ~ Psalm 121:7-8

"Jesus says, Come to me, all of you who are weary and carry heavy burdens, and I will give you rest." ~ Matthew 11:28

"The Lord Himself watches over you! The Lord stands beside you as your protective shade." ~ Psalm 121:5

"Those who trust in the Lord will find new strength. They will soar high on the wings of eagles. They will run and not grow weary. They will walk and not faint." ~ Isaiah 40:31

~ Standing in the need of Prayer ~

"Lord, help me to turn my will and life over to you, so you can transform me. I am grateful I am learning to live a victorious life. I thank you for the freedom to come to you in any times of anxiety. I choose to continue to be open to your guidance, as you speak to my heart and renew my mind. Amen"

~ VALUE ~

"Do not be afraid, for you are precious to the Lord. Peace! Be encouraged! Be strong!
(Daniel 10:19)

Chapter 14

Reclaiming Your Voice ~
Maintaining Healthy Boundaries

"Guard your heart above all else, for it determines the course of your life." (Proverbs 4:23)

Congratulations! You made it this far! While it is almost the end of the book, it may still be the beginning of your healthy process in dealing with passive-aggressive people. Therefore, use these pages to continue your journey and refer often to the bullet points that targeted your heart. It is my prayer that you have gained tools to help you break any strongholds, which are preventing you from moving forward. I know you have received knowledge to empower you to untangle distorted relationships.

Entanglements are toxic and will eventually create a loss of identity and healthy boundary lines. Boundaries are essential to maintaining healthy interpersonal relationships. Many boundaries have already been communicated throughout the material in the book. **Now, I must stress the need for consistency in setting healthy boundaries.** When a person is connected to passive-aggressive people, boundaries are constantly being moved. It is vital you learn to set healthy boundaries, as you speak truth with love. Sisters, personal boundaries are a space around yourself which gives a clear sense of who you are, how you think and what you feel. Boundaries also assist in understanding the unhealthy ways you permit others to treat you. When you have damaged emotions, it is easy to allow boundaries to be broken or moved until they become non-existent.

Damaged and shattered boundaries cause you to take on another person's reality, thereby taking responsibility for their feelings, thoughts or behaviors. The result is controlling other people or allowing others to control you. In addition, whenever you take responsibility for others, there is a tendency to keep people in an immature state. Severely injured boundaries or having no boundaries at all means that others can abuse or wound you emotionally, physically, and spiritually.

When people are repeatedly wounded, walls, or rigid boundaries, are put up to protect and prevent further pain. Whenever we set up our own personal boundaries, it means we know who, or what, to allow into our physical, emotional and relational space. For example, if a co-worker consistently turns their work over to you and you have not understood how to stop that pattern, then you are not setting or protecting personal boundaries.

Dear Ones, personal boundaries are evident and become effective when you learn to treat yourself with respect. Often, because a characteristic of passive-aggressive people is they are "boundary busters," you may feel you have to be overly clear with your words. However, since they do not honor other's healthy boundaries, you are showing respect for yourself in speaking with clarity. It is vital to communicate your personal boundaries. *When you have an ability to say yes or no without letting feelings of guilt, anger or fear prevent you from establishing boundaries, then you are maturing, and stepping out of the "passive-aggressive dance."* Healthy boundaries are sufficient to contain and protect the individual, while also creating a space for others to be allowed in appropriately. When you verbalize your physical, emotional, and spiritual framework, you are activating boundaries. For example, if your neighbor asks you to take her to the mall and you cannot say no without feeling guilty, then you are not protecting your personal boundaries. However, you do not share your thoughts of frustration. Therefore, by not sharing, you are also not protecting your boundary lines.

Sisters, an excellent proactive tool, are to verbalize and establish healthy boundaries when breaking passive-aggressive cycles. If boundaries are inflexible, then relationships will be impacted. Unhealthy boundaries are also important to recognize. Unhealthy boundaries may be non-existent, loose or possibly so rigid they are like solid steel walls. If you have set up rigid boundaries, you may need to resolve unhealed issues in your heart. Rigid boundaries lead to controlling behaviors and decrease opportunities to develop connected and bonded relationships.

Crumbled boundaries are weak, non-existent boundaries or very vague ones, which may lead to manipulation, such as being a "doormat." Loose boundaries may lead to being victimized or thinking as a victim instead of a victor. Usually a person with vague or collapsed boundaries is a conflict avoider, people pleaser, and rescuer and/or may also have fear of abandonment.

When you become angry, mad, or resentful towards others and you do not address these feelings, it can become an inroad for the Enemy to keep you stuck in unresolved wounds. If you are still dealing with any of those emotions, it may be that you need to use your voice (verbalize) and speak up with truth and love. Speaking up creates healthy boundaries, but remember, it is a process. It can be scary and risky to speak the truth, even when done lovingly. Ask the Holy Spirit to help you to speak up and not minimize, or deny, issues which must be dealt with honestly. Be true to yourself. Psalm 139:23 reminds us, *"Search me, O God, and know my heart; test me and know my anxious thoughts."* Fears must be addressed in order to be consistent with relational boundaries.

Boundary Fears:

Fears which Prevent honoring personal boundaries:
~ Fear of being seen as selfish by others.
~ Fear of hurting other people's feeling.
~ Fear of rejection and increasing conflict.

Fears which Block honoring other's boundaries:
~ Fear people will take advantage of them.
~ Fear that they will become invisible and give permission for others to control them.
~ Fear they will not meet other people's expectations.

Setting healthy boundaries will require you to be direct and honest about your opinions and feelings. Assumptions are not the same as expectations. You cannot have expectations of others without having clear and communicated boundaries. Passive-aggressive people have their unspoken boundaries designed so you won't need or expect too much from them. Do you know how to draw the line and set healthy boundaries? One of the best ways to assist you in identifying your boundaries is to pay attention to your emotions. When emotions are intense, shaming, or guilt-ridden in response to something a person said or did to you, it may be a flag that your boundaries are being crossed.

Remember, emotions can be distorted, so look for the repetitive patterns. It is essential to record your boundaries and untangle your thoughts. Then, you will be better able to communicate the boundaries with clarity. It is time to live in freedom and rebuild what the Enemy has taken from you.

~ *FREEDOM to REBUILD* ~

"The Lord will work out His plans for my life; for your faithful love, O Lord, endures forever. Don't abandon me, for you made me." (Psalm 138:8)

I have taken the acronym "Freedom" to use as a foundational tool to enter the rebuilding process. The freedom to maintain your boundaries will keep you from relapsing into old patterns. Wisdom, courage and serenity are required to know what you can change and what you cannot. Healthy boundaries will create healthy relationships. Walking in freedom will involve appropriately identifying, honoring and respecting your needs, feeling, and opinions.

F ~ Free to admit your emotions, such as, fear, anger, disappointment and hurt. The two words which will make a difference in setting healthy boundaries are *consistency* and *commitment.* . Remember to, *"Guard your heart above all else, for it determines the course of your life." (Proverbs 4:23)* **Therefore, to be free it is essential to:**
- Confront issues as close to the event as possible, since passive-aggressive people have selective memory. If you wait too long they may see you, as being argumentative, frequently seeing you as the "**enemy.**" When the passive-aggressive person sees you as the enemy, it will be hard to take ownership of their actions and behaviors, due to blaming patterns.
- Deal with one behavior at a time. Passive-aggressive people learn to have short attention spans and will act like they are overwhelmed.
- Use "**time-outs**" verses engaging in destructive cycles. When you begin reacting in the same manner as the passive-aggressive person, you have just been entrapped. Step away and make your time-out purposeful. Use any of the journaling process tools, described earlier in the book, instead of going away to stir-up your negative emotions.
- Choose to stop rationalizing harmful cycles.

R ~ Renew your mind and develop a new way of thinking. Realize you may have codependent patterns and replace your "**reactions**" with "**healthy responses**." There is no longer an option to stay blind, once you have faced reality. You must heal. Ask yourself, *"Am I now trying to win the approval of men, or of the Heavenly Father? Am I trying to please men?" (Galatians 1:10)*
Therefore, in renewing the mind it is vital to:

- Stop thinking you can change the passive-aggressive man, by trying harder.
- Stop taking up his slack. He will let you lead as long as you take the responsibility.
- Stop preventing growth consequences of toxic people. Over time the person may resent your leadership.
- Stop taking ownership for the passive-aggressive person's destructive behavior.

E ~ Ensure the safety of yourself and that of your children. Do not hesitate or second guess your course of action. Get out if you feel in danger. God desires that you live in peace and safety. Whenever there is doubt, worry, or anxiety, call on Jehovah Shalom. Jehovah Shalom will show you the path to peace. *"Your ears shall hear a word behind you saying, this is the path, now walk in it." (Isaiah 30:21)* **Therefore, to ensure your safety crucial to:**

- Intentionally develop a proactive plan to provide safety.
- Memorize **phone numbers** of safe places, which may be needed to provide refuge.
- Know names of people, who you may need to call if necessary.
- Realize domestic violence is not to be messed with, rationalized or excused for long periods of time.

E ~ Evaluate and replace any unhealthy boundaries for yourself. The Lord addresses why consistency is important. *"A hot-tempered man will have to pay the penalty. If you rescue him, you will have to do it again." (Proverbs 19: 19)* **Therefore, to evaluate your actions it is necessary to:**

- Clearly state your boundaries.
- State your position if boundaries are being minimized ignored or invalidated.
- Consistently follow through with action steps when boundaries are not honored.
- Honor and respect yourself. Address hurtful nonverbal and verbal messages as close to the event as possible.

D ~ Define your identity through the eyes of the Lord. See yourself as a daughter of the most High God. Remember, you are chosen and you are filled with a purpose. El Roi, is the God that sees you. *"You are a chosen people, a royal priesthood, a holy nation, a people belonging to Father God." (1Peter 2:9)* **Therefore, to define your identity it is important to:**

- Know God wants to lavish on you, which means a never-ending overflow.
- See that God has redeemed you to fulfill your destiny.
- Realize your past does not dictate your future. Yes, it is an influence; however, your test and trial can become a testimony to others.
- Declare who you are as a chosen daughter of the King of Kings.

O ~ Own your own. Acknowledge your own patterns and any fears you may have about your future. Ask yourself if you are a rescuer, or an enabler. If so, purposely break the cycle.

Trust the Lord to deliver you from fears. *"Do not be afraid, for I am with you. Do not be discouraged, for I am your God, I will strengthen you and help you; I will uphold you with my righteous hand." (Isaiah 41:10)* **Therefore, to be true to your journey, a key principle is to:**

- Know the truth, for the truth will set you free.
- Seek the Lord.
- Activate the scriptural principles in your life.
- Believe, the Lord himself will go before you and He will direct your path. Do not remain in a state of discouragement. Take action!

M~ Maintain a healthy supportive network. *"My God is my rock, in whom I find protection; He is my shield, the power that saves me, and my place of safety. He is my refuge, my savior, the one who saves me from violence." (2 Samuel 22:3)* **Therefore, to maintain a healthy network you:**

- Must gather a network of safe people who are trustworthy. They will speak the truth to you in love.

- Must know God did not go to the cross for you to be under any form of abuse.
- Must remember, the Holy Spirit can be a source of strength.
- Must keep hope alive for a brighter future. I encourage you to remain realistic as you are hopeful.

Ladies, you have taken-in a lot throughout these pages. Prayerfully, you have uncovered truth and are on a healthy journey of understanding how to work through the chaos of passive-aggressive relationships. Hopefully, you have begun to journal and untangle the circumstances involved in your journey. As you journal, consider going beyond the basics of tasks and challenges. Write about the enlightenment you are gaining as you dig deep into the issues. Spend time listing your personal restorative tools you are using to bring clarity to unhealthy patterns. Finally, select the intentional steps you choose today that will bring greater personal peace and joy in your relationships.

~ Prayer ~

"For I know the plans I have for you, says the Lord. They are plans for good and not disaster, to give you a future and a hope. In those days when you pray, I will listen. If you look for me in earnest, you will find me when you seek me. I will be found by you, says the Lord." (Jeremiah 29:11-13)

Chapter 15

Passive-Aggressive Connections ~
Removing the Blinders

"If you need wisdom, ask our generous God, and He will give it to you. . . ." (James 1:5)

When I meet with single women connected with passive-aggressive men, there is one thread which surfaces time and time again; potential. Women who work with, date or invest a lot of time in passive-aggressive relationships, generally talk about the sweet man and all the potential he encompasses. They know, and rehearse in their minds, how they can help this man to grow-up. At first, they do not see passive-aggressive behavior. They only see the "cute man." Most of the time there are subtle signs of hurtful behaviors. However, the women do not know it is covert hostility (passive aggression) brooding just under the surface. So, they are under the illusion that, they can affect change in the man with love and encouragement. However, by the time they see the passive-aggressive behaviors emerge they are in love and find it difficult to pull back and assess the reality. They are forever, hopeful that love will win out; they find they are going deeper into the relationship.

Over time these ladies become disappointed and yet, feel they have devoted a great deal of emotional commitment into the relationship. They falsely sense that, "*just around the corner, things will change. After all, last week, he was so nice and spoke so tenderly to me."* These types of words, replay in women's minds a thousand times over. Even though, each time they are attempting to keep hope alive. Although these women try to keep the relationship moving in a positive direction, one day the pressure of the relationship becomes too much and that same woman snaps. When she has had enough of the emotional abuse she finally realizes, something has to give. She must break from the snares and traps.

As I mentioned before, it's completely possible for people to finally get off the passive-aggressive merry-go-round. After reality sets in, the women must grieve the loss of dreams, hopes, and expectations. It is imperative to not only heal from their broken-ness, but they have to reframe and reinvest in their future life. If they do not take this step, they will merely select another man who is unhealthy or another passive aggressor. Next, it is vital for women to guard against the hardening of their hearts and not clump all men as the same.

The married women, who were torn between loving the Dr. Hyde, yet fearful of Dr. Jekyll, have got to also find their voice (verbalize) to break from the snares of silence. Women connected to passive-aggressive men are fearful of the outbursts and rage underneath the pleasant exterior which is presented to the world. So often, within my office, I heard the countless stories not told to anyone before. With timid voices, *"If I tell someone, I know I will be blamed for the negativity. Most people think he is not the kind of man who would have rage."* The outside world sees this person as charming and ser-vant-hearted. Women tell me they have heard people say *"She is so lucky to have so and so in her life. He is always so sweet and willing to do anything for anybody. He has such a servant-heart."*

These women tell me how the turmoil is so mind-boggling; they feel as if they have lost their ever-loving mind. They begin saying things like, *"Could this be the same man I connected with in my youth?"* Like many women, in their view, this man is long gone.

However, truth be known, this is the same man who simply had buried their passive-aggressive tendencies and character.

~ THE CONNECTION ~

The age old question which emerges out of the lips of women after passive-aggressive patterns become clearer is, *"How in the world did I ever get connected with this man?"*

- **Innocence**: If you were a person who simply could not believe that people could be devious, conniving or manipulative, then denial is a tactic the enemy used to keep you in darkness with a passive-aggressive person. If you did not come out of a chaotic family system yourself, you are blindsided by the passive-aggressive behavior.

- **Super Responsible**: If you are a person who gives people the benefit of the doubt over and over again, you will fall into the trap of the passive-aggressive person and become a rescuer. You will become overly conscientious. This is a tactic the Enemy will use to have you excuse and rationalize the passive-aggressive behavior and patterns.

- **Lacking Boldness**: If you are a person whose self-talk brings you down or causes self doubt, then the Enemy will prey on your mind. Self doubt leads to a lack of self worth and then the Enemy can march right in your life and slander your identity.

- **Over-Analyzing**: If you are a person who tries to get to the root of situations, you will overcompensate for the passive-aggressive person. You have taken on the role of picking up the slack from the passive-aggressive person. You think, "this person has been so hurt in their past," you can't bring yourself to hurt them anymore. You have missed the truth that the Word says, speak the truth in love. You begin making excuses for the passive-aggressive person which leads to dead end streets. No change will occur, because you are taking control in an attempt to stop the drama and attacks.

- **Christian Submission**: As a Christian, you may have been taught to submit in an unhealthy manner. You were shamed if you tried to use your voice to expose the behaviors at home. Other times, pastors may have stated that you may be blowing things out of proportion or acting like a victim. This belief silences many women who do not want to appear rebellious. The Enemy will tap into these religious distortions, and play on the internal messages of you not wanting to let God, boss, family or the church, down. Therefore, you become performance based to mask your emotional wounds.

- **False Optimism**: If you are a person who is optimistic beyond what you see, feel and think, somehow, you see a legitimate reason to keep hoping for a change. The Enemy will capitalize on you not walking in the facts or truth. The longer you stay in blindness, the more susceptible you become to passive-aggressive relationships. Why do you stay in blindness? One of the reasons is due to the glimpses of positive times when you are with the passive-aggressive person. You get this little change from that person and you want to believe there is a greater change coming. Well, it does, but it will not last but a short time.

- **Familiarity**: If you were a person who grew up in a home of unrest and emotional distance, constant verbal fights, or addictive environments, you may be familiar with emotional and relational chaos. It becomes a comfortable place and you more easily accept the passive-aggressive behaviors.

- **Lack of Role Models**: Repeating the script of your family roles is comfortable because you feel its part of your identity. If you had a mother who was an enabler, or caregiver, yet strong and independent, you need to be careful. You may be following in her steps. Don't get me wrong, being compassionate and a giver when in balance is not unhealthy. That is called the gift of mercy and giving. However, when out of balance, this creates a mind set of excusing and fixing other people's problems, which is called, co-dependency. This is an attractive trait to a passive-aggressive person.

- **Rewrite the Dramatic Script**: If you are a person who was hoping to rewrite the script of your family system, you may attempt, but not have the right tools to do it. You attempt to not repeat the same behaviors, yet find yourself duplicating the same patterns until reality seemingly smacks you in the face.

- **Spoken and Unspoken Family of Origin Rules**: You may be someone who was not allowed to talk about family rules. You needed to "Suck it up and stop whining." You were taught to ignore when someone is raising their voice at you. The family's needs were usually placed before your personal needs and you become good at burying your hurt. The Enemy is given a doorway to enter when this behavior is in place and the role with the passive-aggressive person seems to feel a lot like the childhood years. This is not to say, we should not care for others. However, there must be balance.

Dear Daughters of the Lord, you will experience blessings, as you continue to put your hope in the Lord. Your Heavenly Father, Elohim will remain faithful to you, while you become skilled at resting and abiding in Him in during the struggles. (Psalm 146:5-6)

~ HOPE and HEALING is POSSIBLE ~

As you work through your own processing, also realize the passive-aggressive person is working through theirs as well. If they gain understanding and see the changes within you, there is hope they will thrive and be able to leave behind their toxic behavior. In Christ, you have hope for honest change. I know the Lord heals, restores and refreshes relationships. There is no personality flaw too big for our Lord to sift through and heal. Therefore, I want to share a very personal letter from one of my clients. He is a man who admitted his passive-aggressive behaviors and was able to take a journey toward wholeness. This gentleman walked the journey to break generational cycles of passive aggression and has the following letter to share. Yes, ladies, it is possible for your relationships to be redeemed and restored, if the passive-aggressive person walks through the healing process.

"I have been married 34 years. My wife and two daughters are radiantly beautiful in body, soul and spirit. They embody the glory of God. They are the incarnate of the beauty of God. They are the crown of Creation. They are women through and through and exactly the way God designed them. Through God, they give life to the world and this is true of all women. As daughters of God, you hold a special place in His heart and beauty is core to your heart. Beauty is one of the most powerful pictures of God on this earth; it inspires, it nourishes and it comforts, it is strong and it can be fierce.

This has not always been my conscience thought. For my journey with Christ has been a long, painful and fearful healing process due to my passive-aggressive behaviors and patterns. Mine is a story of God's relentless pursuit so that I can move into the priestly position in my home and family, where He reigns and where I submit to what He wants. During this journey, God also placed within my heart a passion for other Christian men who also have been passive aggressive; and on whose behalf I also write this letter.

First and foremost, I want to apologize for all passive-aggressive men, to all women who have been hurt by us. I realize, as passive-aggressive men, we have messed up big time. Adam's failure to stand in the gap for Eve sent a horrific shock wave through human history. Adam's failure has become my failure, which threatened to destroy the very foundation of my marriage and family. Unfortunately, in some cases those relationship have been broken and others are completely destroyed. The pain and suffering inflicted by our behavior, as men, is beyond measure. I know that now. However, it is not beyond the healing and restorative power of our Lord and Savior. What Adam lost, and what is for us to regain through Christ Jesus, are life rhythms, or pillars, that use to pulsate in the veins of man before the fall.

What we failed to bring to women, in our relationships, is the provisionary heart of a servant warrior who looks ahead and watches over his family, and provides protection. As a servant warrior, I want to impart compassion and mercy to my family and others. A man who is under authority from the Lord will be able to break the shackles of past bondages. Instead, as passive aggressive men, we did nothing, became tyrants, or fell somewhere in between.

What we failed to bring to you was a protective heart of a tender warrior who shields, defends, guards and stands in the gap, but who also is a fierce warrior equipped to shatter strong-holds. Instead many of us were brutes and bullies.

What we failed to bring to you is a teaching heart of a wise mentor who models, explains, disciples and guides. We are supposed to know life skills, but we did not have personal models to learn the tools to function in healthy ways. Instead we either acted as "know-it-alls" or "know-nothings."

What we failed to bring to you is a loving, faithful heart of a friend, a lover, who is compassionate and who stands with you. God is love, and is one who listens with a heart who wants to deeply really know you. Instead, as passive-aggressive men, we were betrayers.

We men, have a lot of repenting to do before our God and in front of our families. But our God is a God of restoration. That is why you can never lose hope for your relationship. Christ came to heal the broken-hearted and to set the captives free. We are all the broken hearted, but he has set us free on a journey of recovery through Him. Oh yes, there will be trouble, but you must be persistent and we will learn to walk with God through this, and the healing will come.

You are probably asking what it was in my family history that brought about my passive-aggressive behavior. What went wrong?

This is not the way it was suppose to be. First and foremost, fear was the driving force for my behavior. The origin of that fear trails back to my family history and can be found in the messages and father wounds I experienced as a boy. Verbal arrows fired with deadly accuracy impacting specific places on my heart that contained the strength placed there by God; and our Enemy was waiting for the right time.

Then the first message was fired when I was yet a still young boy, "You can't do anything right," and then the messages kept coming; all through my teenage years and through college, "You're not capable of doing it correctly. You'll never get it right and, can't you think?" Instantly a vow was made deep within my heart: "I will never be like my father, successful, wealthy and a perfectionist." The vow became an agreement, a stronghold from the Enemy to shut me down and take me out of God's plan. From that vow, a false self developed and lies became the truth to me. I decided in my heart that I was not capable of having good relationships. My list went like this: I was not a good person, I was a criminal, I couldn't do anything right, I was not a man. Don't ask me to perform, because I have nothing to offer. This became my belief system about who I was.

Certainly, I did not want anyone to see this side of me, so I created a false image for the general public. I became someone who could strike a pose as whatever the world needed me to be. I let people see just enough to make them think they can trust me. I did enough just to get by on a daily basis. All of this was driven by the fear of failure. Really, I was afraid people would find out that I was really already a failure in my mind. Procrastination became my behavior pattern. It also was the method by which I would sabotage my relationships; especially with my wife and children. All this resulted in sabotaging my priestly position in our home. I would put things off and then never come through, which all lead to chaos and destruction. Why? Because if I did follow through, they will find out that I am actually not capable, trustworthy, or honest. So, I would say yes, when I meant no. However, all this was counterfeit to what is true about me. Remember the strengths of my heart that contained the wounds from the message of the arrows? They are faith, trust, leadership and courage. That's who I really am. That is what God meant for me.

Faith kept me enough in the truth to allow me to cry out to God for healing of these wounds. The personal vows I made early in life could then be brought to the surface. I could see how the agreements kept me bound up and in shackles. It was only with Christ walking alongside me that I was able to face the pain of having an earthly father from whom I would never receive the blessing of his love, affirmation and validation as to who I am. That understanding gave me the strength to run to my heavenly Father and receive Christ as my Savior, and then set me on a healing journey.

I entered a process of restoration of my true heart, which finds me 28 years later, and able to write this letter. I can affirmatively state, I have moved into a priestly position in my home. The journey is, by far, not over. There is more healing and restoration ahead and likely I will make more mistakes. Regardless, there is one promise God has firmly placed on my heart: I will never ever abandon my post next to my wife and children as her husband and as their father, as God meant it to be for His kingdom purposes.

Beloved of God, don't ever lose heart. I know there are men everywhere going through similar break through journeys and being restored to priestly positions in their homes. How? Jesus Christ came to heal the broken hearted and set the captives free. Each one of them realized they needed to give Christ permission to walk with them down to the wounded places in their hearts to find healing. As in my journey, their restoration process will likely need to include professional counseling with experience in all forms of physiological behavior and who also understand the nature of spiritual warfare along with Christ's redemptive power. In fact, not only did I, but my wife and children began counseling with Dee, to help us navigate the long, painful restoration and forgiveness journey. Don't let anyone tell you it's not possible.

I'd also like to say to you men, who find yourselves a drift in chaos in your homes, with strained broken relationships with your wife and children, quit whining and blaming others. Your Abba Father is speaking to you through the chaos, and He is saying that the instability in your homes is because your life rhythms are out of whack. They are distorted by lies and false perceptions grown by vows, and then agreements you made early on about who you are. You must know who you really are, as known by God. You must also know who your enemy is, and you must understand who God is. You cannot do this by your own strength. You can only do it by surrendering to Christ. You can only do it by walking with God. However, it will still require you to make the decision to move to open that door. Jesus will not break down the door to your heart. You must give Him permission to come in. Ah, when you open that door, Jesus will rush in and behind Him will be an army of heavenly hosts fit for battle on your behalf.

Beloved of God, your Abba Father knows what is on your heart. He does hear your prayers. He even bends down close to you when you pray. He hears your cries. He weeps with you. He has never left your side. You need not look up; just turn your head to either side, for there you will find He stands, right next to you. He stands ready to re-awaken your heart by His healing hands. You need to draw closer to Him. You need to walk with Him. You need to know that the battle is His. You need to know that there is hope in your relationships.

I am honored to write this letter and will continue prayer for your healing relationships. If I can step out of passive-aggressive behavior and into the loving arms of honest family relationships guided by God, it is possible for you and those you love. I'll close with this prayer: Dear Abba Father, I thank you for guiding me through my journey to freedom and restoration. I choose to declare and proclaim my healing from being shackled in fear. Thank you for helping me to understand my new healthy boundaries. I choose to praise you as I continue in healthy relationships. Amen."

Tears have fallen down the faces of women, as the letter was read, at various seminars and retreats I have facilitated over the years. I am grateful to the men and women who have chosen to break free from the bondage of passive aggression.

~ THE VOICES of LESSONS LEARNED ~

Sisters, it is always good to hear from those who have gone before you. Women who have walked the path of deliverance and transformation are able to share their testimonies to assist others to be set free. I encourage you to walk with other women who are blind to the traits and tendencies of passive-aggressive people. The psychological world frequently offers little hope for the healing of a passive-aggressive personality. However, with God, it is possible if people are choosing to walk out the complete healing process. Although, I must state loud and clear, that healing obviously will not happen overnight and involves you taking a lot of time and energy to engage in your own healing process.

The following are a list of strategies and lessons learned from other women who have gone before you and are now living trans-formed lives. It is my privilege to pass on their truth born out of the struggle to break their silent cry. It is their desire to be silent no more!

- Grieve the idealistic dreams of your marriage or significant passive-aggressive relationships.
- Take time to heal yourself, regardless of whether the pas-sive-aggressive person chooses to change or not.
- Give testimony to others of how God has sustained you in your journey.
- Connect and be accountable with safe people who speak life into your heart when discouragement rises. Community is extremely important. Get a life outside the painful and oppressive environment.
- Know that the Lord will fight your battle.

- Recognize that Satan will use your husband, boss, family and friends to bring warfare into your life. Declare that you more than a conqueror and are on the winning side.
- Become a prayer warrior and seek to understand the role of the Holy Spirit in your healing journey.
- Own your own issues and keep your conscious clear from bitterness which is poisonous to your mind and soul.
- Do the internal work to press on in the *"letting go"* process, which will prevent hardening of the heart.
- Learn and practice setting healthy boundaries.
- Connect with a safe person so you can just off load, without un-loading on them. Safe people can give validation and be objective in bringing clarity to your reality. They can pray for your strength and courage to keep it moving forward.
- Heal from any co-dependent behaviors to rescue, fix, and people please.
- Seek counseling when appropriate. If you have moved from hurt to anger to resentment to bitterness and are stuck, then it is time to reach out for help.
- Realize that your husband, boss, friend, family member may not want to change. However, do not let that stop you from implementing tools to live victoriously.
- Do not permit abuse to continue. The Christian community has a hard time believing there is such a thing as emotional and verbal abuse.
- Help other women to recognize signs of emotional abuse.
- Get a vision for the future and walk in it.
- If you have children, be very careful not to make them feel responsible for your unhappiness. It can split their loyalty. Don't make children emotional spouses. The burden is not theirs to carry. They must also unlock their own hurts from the passive-aggressive environmental impact.
- Remember in your worst moments, God is right there.
- Be realistic in your perceptions. The angels will stand guard over you. Whenever you receive cards, calls, prayers from others; you should record these blessings. You then have

an opportunity to do the same for others in your sphere of influence.

- Do not trivialize your reality.
- We have to remove the barriers in the church community by using our voices to break this insidious form of covert aggression, in order for other women to be healed.
- We have got to be about the Father's business. We have been touched by God and we can touch others by speaking the truth in love. Don't beat yourself up in life. God always has a divine intervention on the way.
- In life, know that we will get hurt and we will have pain. God will be real to you in the "now story." Whatever, your story is "now" the Lord will meet you there.
- Dear sisters, you can't wait to seek restoration and recovery until you are emotionally or physically stable. Start today!

~ Prayer ~

"Abba Father, thank you for victory in my life. Please allow me to continue to see trends in my life and to identify any areas which may require healing. I pray you will equip me to be bold and courageous. I choose to praise you regardless of circumstances. Amen"

Chapter 16

Apprehending Your Destiny ~
Equipped to Walk Victoriously

"For the mountains may move and the hills disappear, but even then my faithful love for you will remain. My covenant of blessings will never be broken, says the Lord, who has mercy on you." (Isaiah 54:10)

The Abba Father has deposited a beautiful package of gifts and potential in you. You are made in His image. It was His pleasure and delight to give you what you need to succeed in life. You have too many gifts, talents and abilities to allow other people or the Enemy to snatch, steal and sabotage the good gifts deposit in you. Whenever you apprehend and take hold of your identity in Christ, even in the midst of adversity, you will rise up from the ashes of abuse. Rise up my sister! Confidence will burst forth and you will rejoice once again and say, "I was born for a purpose and no amount of adversity will stop me from obtaining that purpose." You will need courage and a holy boldness to unwrap the entanglement of the passive-aggressive web. The spiritual warfare you are walking in is part of your destiny and your victory is God's design.

Ladies, I pray you declare that even though you are tied up in the mire of pain, confusion, frustration, or embarrassment, you realize God has not forgotten you. You have not been written off in life.

As a Christian woman, you have favor because of the resurrection power of Jesus. Rest and stand in the victory, while testifying to what God has completed. You are not to be treated abusively, it cost Jesus a lot to give you an inheritance, purpose and freedom. Do you know and believe that God loves you? I know when women have lived with this subtle type of emotional roller coaster; it may be hard to stay in a place of hope. The Abba Father desires that you walk in grace, truth, favor and peace. You are no longer invisible. You are not as powerless as you currently feel today.

I have to say, the hope is not in trying to fix, rescue or excuse the situation. The hope is in the choices you have set in motion to this point. You have already read fifteen chapters of this book, while others may have set it aside. You have taken the time to process this information, while others have not gone beyond the front cover. You have hope, because you are examining who you are and who you were created to be. The hope is in unmasking the reality of your situation and putting it in the light. The hope is in choosing life and not emotional, relational or spiritual death. The hope is in stopping the denial. The hope is on the other side of grief and letting go of what you cannot control. The hope is in doing the things you do have control over, in a healthy and productive way. My sister, take off the shackles of oppression, appeasement, fear, false guilt, shame, un-worthiness, intimidation, and doubt. The decisions you make on this healing and deliverance journey must be specifically planned. If you change nothing, then nothing will change.

~ Prayer for the Soul ~

"O Lord, if you heal me, I will be truly healed; if you save me, I will truly be saved. My praises are for you alone." (Jeremiah 17:14) Help me Lord, to discern the truth. I realize the Abba Father wants to show himself to be the strength in my life for eternal purposes. I want to walk in the revelation that God stands ready to do a new thing in my life. He desires that I fan the flame and keep the ambers of hope ignited in my heart. The Lord has the power to bring about a harvest in life, regardless of the adversity I am facing and have

faced in the past. I want to be lead on a path of freedom, healing, renewal, restoration and transformation. I want to tune-in to hear the voice of the Holy Spirit. I know that God will direct me out of the wilderness of emotional abuse. He will heal my mind of confusion and refocus me in due season. Holy Spirit, please remind me of who you are and the destiny I have. No matter what kind of chaotic-drama I feel I walked yesterday, today and tomorrow I will walk in God's plan. AMEN!

The Holy Spirit will make a shift in your life, so you can be free of oppression, suppression and depression. There is an incredible power available to you for the asking. James1: 1- 9 tells us to seek and ask for wisdom. It is a Holy Spirit, appointed time in your life. My sisters, believe He is able to do exceedingly, abundantly above all we can ask or do. God is accessible to all who cry out to Him. The letting go process is one of the steps you will need to work through in order to live in freedom and inner peace.

~ LETTING GO ~

"We are pressed on every side by troubles, but we are not crushed. We are perplexed, but not driven to despair." (2 Corinthians 4:8)

Letting go is a process! Letting go takes love. Letting go of unrealistic expectations and dreams is extremely difficult, but a necessary step towards opening doors to the future. It is so important to understand when, and what, to let go of and how to let go. It is essential to practice letting go in order to live in the present, and move towards the future. Letting go is a process of taking small steps. Change may be a struggle as you face reality head on. When you become aware of what to let go, it will help to decrease reactionary responses to triggering situations. Therefore, clarity replaces confusion and chaos. Awareness ultimately gives way to new options, new choices and new perspectives. I have come to understand that letting go will be dealt with on a physical, spiritual, and emotional level.

- **Physical:** There will be two physical challenges. One involves the fact that many women relay dealing with passive aggression frequently leaves them physically ill. The other physical change is the hostile environmental space becomes a place of walking on egg shells. If you are in a marital relationship, you may be in the same house, but live as roommates. There is a physical loss when this happens. The things you would normally share become stifled by defense mechanisms.

- **Spiritually**: There is a spiritual isolation within the faith-based community because of the silence. Unfortunately, it has been difficult to find safe people who understand the nature and behavioral cycles of passive aggression. Women have shared, that as a result of isolation, they often feel shame or guilt. There is also disillusionment as to how to respect the partner when there is a lack of priestly leadership.

- **Emotional**: The shock of having to deal consistently with an erratic relationship is emotionally draining. Hurt, disappointment, frustration, irritation, minimizing, avoidance and lack of resolution over time, will take an emotional toll on a person.

*Power Tool: *"When a person is worn down emotionally, physically and spiritually, something must change. Without change, you feel like you are losing your mind. Exposing the problem in order to resolve a problem involves a path of letting go. Learning to let go means awareness and acknowledgement of attitudes and actions. Learn to speak from your heart and speak the truth. The healing is going to take time as you reframe a new reality. So, my sister, take as much time as you need to walk out the healing journey."*

Let go and let God's miracle touch heal you as you journey through the process of letting go. Surrendering and letting go is not a passive action of giving up, being a doormat, lying down and doing nothing. However, it is about coming to terms with what is not healthy. It is important to know when to hold and when to let go, in order to stop stepping into a passive-aggressive dance. The tool of surrendering what is not working will require strength, courage, commitment and faith. *My sisters, what you resist taking actions on, will continue to persist.*

Praying, believing and listening are all a part of surrender. Staying stuck in a destructive cycle and responding the same way over and over again leads to frustration. If you are expecting different results from the same actions, you are one step away from insanity. Letting go will put the present reality into perspective. You will need patience, acceptance, resilience and understanding. These are key factors involved in learning to detach. Detachment is part of letting go and breaking passive-aggressive cycles. The tool of taking one day at a time will prove to be a strategic key in the process of letting go and receiving emotional, physical and spiritual freedom.

Letting Go ~ Keys to Healthy Detachment

Letting go is defined as:
- Choosing to make a change regardless of fear and the risk.
- Choosing to let go of false guilt.
- Accepting the losses in life and taking time to grieve.
- Accepting personal responsibility for your actions and your part in a passive-aggressive dance.
- Choosing to step out of denial.
- Choosing to release anger, resentment and bitterness towards others.

Barriers to letting go:
- Fear which says, "If I let go, then I will fall apart." "I have to stay strong for my children." "I don't have time to grieve."
- Fear of rejection, "If I let go, then they won't like me."
- Fear of being judged or disapproved of by others.
- Fear of the unknown.
- Fear others will be angry.
- Fear of injustice and having others blame you for the relational problems.

- Fear, if I practice letting go, then things will fall apart without your intervention.
- Fear of conflict intensifying and becoming defensive.
- Fear of not getting personal needs met.
- Fearful of being seen as disloyal.

Steps to letting go:
First, you must identify what needs to be let go:
- Fear, grief, anger, resentment
- Resistance to change
- **Write out anything else you fear in the process.**

Next, define the obstacles you have to letting go:
- Lack of confidence in self and fear of conflict
- Inability to express emotions
- Over-dependence or avoidance
- **Write any additional obstacles you can identify in letting go.**

Lastly, stop procrastinating and activate your tools.
- Understand why you are putting it off
- Describe the cost of not letting go
- Describe the benefit of letting go
- **Review what the outcomes have been in the past by procrastinating.**

~ *Letting Go Takes Love and Commitment* ~

Letting go will require love and commitment. As we let go, it doesn't mean we don't have concern or care about other people. However, it does mean that we are not to do things for other people which they can do for themselves. When we choose to let go, we make a conscious decision not to enable others to continue toxic or destructive cycles. It does mean allowing others to grow from experiencing their own consequences. To let go means, we do not fix, prevent, rescue or make excuses for unhealthy patterns. Letting go means we stop protecting others from learning from their actions. However, we remain supportive while setting healthy boundaries.

When we purposely let go, then others learn to face the reality of their decisions, behaviors and patterns. To let go also means, we do not shame or judge others. However, we learn to speak the truth with Christ-like love, while remembering our own human failures. This means we allow the Holy Spirit to search our own human defects and intentionally correct them. Learning to let go will require being focused and intentional each day, while treasuring one day at a time. It will mean doing the next healthy and right thing which leads to freedom and victory. You will grow and become more accountable and learn to heal the past and look forward to the future. Letting go paves the path to apprehending your unique and valued identity. When you maintain your commitment to letting go of hurts, fears, unhealthy behaviors, disappointments and lost dreams, it leads to a distinct walk towards healing. It opens the doors to choose to love and forgive, which sets you free to be all that, *"The Lord"* has designed you to be. Selah.

Psalm 91: 15 says, *"When they call on me, I will answer; I will be with them in trouble. I will rescue and honor them."* Indeed, God hears your prayers. Aren't you glad about that? This should cause a holy boldness in you and add pep to your step. God will establish that which He decrees. His word will never go void. Therefore, walk in confidence that you have Him directing your steps and that if you ask anything according to His will, He hears you. If you know He hears you, whatever you ask, you can believe that He will release it in your lives. You have now received many tools for your toolkit.

~ TRIUMPH in CHRIST ~

We have triumph through Christ. It is important to give thanks to our Abba Father for leading us in the eternal triumph regardless of the circumstances we get ourselves into. The Lord, promises to always escort us into glorious victory. That means, no matter what we are facing, no matter what's going on in the world around us, no matter what anybody says, no matter what people do or don't do, no matter what losses we experience, we are actually more than conquerors. We are more than our circumstances.

In the middle of adversity or tough times, we can rejoice. He will supply exactly what you need when you need it. Seek the kingdom of the Lord and He will be near and will add to the newly found faith you have. It may be faith as small as a mustard seed, and God will still honor it. Watch the Abba Father grow that mustard seed faith. We can declare and claim there will be cause for a victory celebration. We can trust that God is actively working in our lives, as we continue to walk in faith. Be expectant my sister. When things don't look good in the natural, remember, you serve a supernatural God. With God leading us into freedom, we can always plan for liberty. We can plan for restoration to take place. We can plan for a comeback that will make us stronger and better than we ever were before!

~ Prayer ~

"Heavenly Father, I give you thanks and praise today for the promise. For you are faithful and steadfast. You will never leave, nor forsake me. The Lord is near. Continue to give me your vision for the future, so that I will press on confidently into the abundant life you have for me and my family. In Jesus Name, I pray." Amen.

God is not Finished ~ Stay the Course

Dear Sisters,

You are victorious! By reaching the end of this book, you have journeyed beyond the multitudes of people who begin, but do not walk fully in their journey. I am so proud of you and it is time to celebrate your persistence. It is my fervent prayer that you experienced a Holy Spirit release and refreshment while reading this book. The Abba Father wants you to walk in liberty and deliverance from being under the yoke of oppression and suppression. I pray that you, as daughters of the King of Kings, have been strengthened and equipped while you found rest for your soul and were set free from the snares of the enemy of mankind, Satan.

Beloved sisters, continue to remember, you are chosen and highly valued women of God. You are worthy to be treated with honor. You are worthy to be cherished! It is just waiting to be ignited. No longer are you walking as invisible, voiceless oppressed or abused women; trying to fake it until you make it. That is not your Abba Father's design for you. No! There is purpose and destiny in you, waiting to be fulfilled.

My sisters, Isaiah 60: 1-3 lets us know the Lord is calling you. It is time to arise and shine! Your light has come and the glory of the Lord surrounds you. The Word encourages us to believe we are to rise up from the depression, oppression, abuse and walk a new life!

You can shine and be radiant with the glory of the Lord. God calls you His "baby girl." He wants to anoint your voice to speak boldly, to have your mind unshackled, to plant your feet on solid ground as you live in liberty and deliverance. He wants to release, refresh, and refocus you to press forward and finish this earthy race.

Yes! This is a new day and a new season and you must declare the promises of the Almighty God. Woman come alive, wake up, step up and march into your fullest potential. Throw off the shackles of shame; throw off the poverty mentality which says, "This must the best there is for me. I might as well settle for what I have." No! My sister, the Lord God, Jehovah wants to lavish on you. Lavish means a never ending outpour of grace. A perpetual flow! God wants to lavish on us. (Set aside a time to read Ephesians 1:7-8)

It is time to get it straight. It is time to live in the love and favor of the Lord. When a person lives in an oppressive environment, hopes, dreams, and visions may be snatched and squashed. But, oh glory, I pray you will come out of the dead places and walk with a new pep in your step, with your head held high. For you are worthy! Fight for your faith and healing.

As you have let go of old behaviors and unhealthy thinking, the Holy Spirit is able to birth a new hope and sense of greater purpose in you. Prepare and pray that you will receive knowledge, wisdom and discernment from the Holy Spirit in order to live an abundant life. God is not finished, so I encourage you to intentionally stay the course.

Standing Shield to Shield with you, *Dariel Brown (Dee)*

Addendum ~
Safety and Strategies and Biblical
Rights when Abuse is Involved

"He has sent me, Jesus, to heal the brokenhearted . . . and to set at liberty those who are bruised." (Luke 4:18)

There are passive-aggressive men, who are also hot-tempered. If the passive-aggressive relationship escalates to becoming physically abusive, whether it's one, or one hundred times, the impact of physical abuse breeds intimidating, paralyzing fear. Domestic violence strikes all races and ethnic groups and surfaces in various denominations. The church is filled with people who have the propensity to be violent. This is sad, but true. My sisters, if you have established healthy boundaries to protect yourself and your children, or have decided to vacant the premises, this is a dangerous time for you. Many violent abusers are threatened by you getting stronger and becoming healed. They are comfortable with the way things have been and hate the change of your healthy boundaries. Their own insecurities make them feel scared that you will leave and they will lose control over you. So, this next information is to equip you with a few tools. However, I encourage you to connect with a safe person and connect to the domestic violence organizations in your area. You must decide if you fear for your life, to get out. Stop making rationalizations to stay. If there is violence, get out now.

"An angry man starts fights; a hot-tempered person commits all kinds of sin." (Proverbs 29:22)

Action Plan ~ Safety Strategies

- Make sure you have more than one set of car house keys hidden, but easily accessible.
- Make sure you have packed a suitcase of clothing and kid's comfort toys.
- Make sure you have extra medication packed.
- Collect the following items and store them at a trusted person's house:
    1. All medical records for you and children
    2. Copy of unpaid bills, credit cards statements
    3. Bank account information
    4. Copies of financial papers, investments, 401k, retirement funds
    5. Documentation of any criminal records
    6. Police reports
    7. Insurance policy numbers
    8. Copy of pay stubs; include yours
    9. Social security information for yourself and children
    10. Cash
    11. All private journals
    12. Current photo of abuser, children and one of yourself
    13. Cherished items, such as pictures
    14. Deeds and other legal records
    15. Birth certificates, visas and passports
    16. Address book with current addresses, phone numbers and e-mails
- Collect emergency numbers and memorize as many as possible.
- Know exactly where you can go and how you will get there if you need to leave in an emergency.
- Know contact numbers and names of people at children's school.
- Open a saving account and start saving a little each month.
- Determine the method of alerting children to call 911.
- Educate yourself before an attack.
- Attend a support group for battered women.
- Remove home address from personal checks.

- Obtain a post office box and submit a change of address in order to have your mail sent to the post box.
- Save all evidence which can prove there has been violence. For example, pictures of broken chairs, ripped clothing or holes in the walls.
- Make a list of the following numbers for emergencies.
    1. Domestic Violence crisis hotline
    2. Battered Women's and Women with Children's Shelter
    3. Local police number or emergency numbers such as 911
    4. Organizations such as Salvation Army
- Make sure you know what to do for legal protection in the county you live. The legal protection such as a restraining order may need to be put in place.

"Getting wisdom is the wisest thing you can do! And whatever else you do, develop good judgment." (Proverbs 4:7)

Acknowledging Biblical Rights of Christian Women

- Biblically, you have a right to set boundaries and speak the truth in love. *"We will speak the truth in love, growing in every way more and more like Christ. . . "* Ephesians 4:15

- Biblically, no one should shut you down from fulfilling your destiny and using your spiritual gifts, talents and abilities. *"God has given each of you a gift from his great variety of spiritual gifts. Use them well to serve one another."* 1 Peter 4:10

- Biblically, you have the right to leave an abusive relationship. *"A prudent person foresees danger and takes precautions. The unwise go blindly on and suffer consequences."* Proverbs 27:12

- Biblically you have a right to be in emotionally, physically, spiritually safe relationships. *"Do not be afraid, for I am with you; do not be discouraged, for I am your God. I will strengthen you and help you; I will hold you up with my victorious right hand."* Isaiah 41:10

About the Author ~

Dee Brown is a life coach, therapist, adult educator, and certified human behavior consultant. She holds a BSN in Behavioral Science and Nursing, Masters Degree in Counseling and Theology. A seasoned national and international speaker, teaching in the US, United Kingdom, Zambia, Republic of South Africa, South Africa, Central Asia and Canada. Dee is a retreat and conference speaker, who has a reputation for her down-to-earth style, candid presentation and sense of humor.

Dee is the CEO/ founder of Cornerstone Coaching Center, a multi-purpose international enterprise with a unique ministry focus on the journey to wholeness. As a Life Coach and Certified Human Behavior Consultant, she has a passion to equip and inspire people to live triumphantly, tap their creative abilities, maximize potential, and fulfill their Divine life purpose. Cornerstone Coaching Center offers business and executive coaching. One of the goals is to teach and equip individuals and organizations to recognize and eliminate sabotaging patterns. Her trainings assist groups and individuals to excel and experience passionate and victorious living.

A multi-cultural understanding allows Dee to work as a trainer in diverse communities, both culturally and multi-denominationally. She has an apostolic call to ignite a fire by equipping and training churches to develop relationally safe, transforming, restorative communities, both nationally and internationally. Brown's goal is to pass on a ray of hope, regardless of a person's circumstances and provide an opportunity for people to be free to pursue their destiny.

Dee has been a pastoral consultant, ministering and teaching a variety of *"Victorious Living"* seminars and classes, such as: Breaking generational strongholds and bondages, Spiritual gifts, Spiritual warfare, Leadership and Team Development, Lay counseling and Transformational recovery ministries, since 1978. She has facilitated and trained others to lead recovery/support groups. Dee has had a private counseling practice for over twenty five years.

As an adult educator, she has taught college-level mental health courses, authored several training materials focusing on holistic health. While teaching in the Washington State Penal systems, she developed curricula addressing; life skills, addiction recovery, grief and loss process, anger management, abuse awareness, conflict and communication skills, wellness and family system dynamics.

Brown is the Co-Founder of Educate Success, an international program designed to identify and eliminate barriers, which prevent sustained personal and professional success.

She is a founding board member of several organizations that all serve as ministry resources and training networks. Dee is a member of: American Association for Christian Counselors; Black African American Association for Christian Counselors; Puget Sound Coaching Association and Northwest Christian Network for Sexual Health.

Books: *Victorious Living Series*

- **Standing Victoriously in The Battle** ~ Demystifying Spiritual Warfare
- **Weapons to Stand Boldly and Win the Battle** ~ Spiritual Warfare Demystified
- **Breaking Passive Aggressive Cycles** ~ The Silent Cry of Christian Women

To contact the author, please write:

Cornerstone Coaching Center, Dee Brown
11417 124th Ave NE ~ Suite 202
Kirkland, WA 98033

DB.Cornerstone@verizon.net
www.coachdbrown.com
www.educatesuccess.com

Please include your story, or the help you received from this book, when writing. Your prayer requests and praise reports are always welcome.

CPSIA information can be obtained
at www.ICGtesting.com
Printed in the USA
BVHW07s1249010818
523277BV00005B/289/P

Shadows, Darkness, and Dawn

Dear brothers and sisters in Christ:
the early church observed with great devotion
 the days of our Lord's passion and resurrection,
and it became the custom of the Church that before the Easter celebration
there should be a forty-day season of spiritual preparation.
During this season converts to the faith were prepared for Holy Baptism.
It was also a time when persons who had committed serious sins
 and had separated themselves from the community of faith
  were reconciled by penitence and forgiveness,
 and restored to participation in the life of the Church.
In this way the whole congregation was reminded
 of the mercy and forgiveness proclaimed in the gospel of Jesus Christ
  and the need we all have to renew our faith.
I invite you, therefore, in the name of the Church,
 to observe a holy Lent:
 by self-examination and repentance;
 by prayer, fasting, and self-denial;
 and by reading and meditating on God's Holy Word.
To make a right beginning of repentance,
 and as a mark of our mortal nature,
 let us now kneel before our Creator and Redeemer.

      —The United Methodist Book of Worship